WISDOM
LIFE'S GREAT TREASURE

WISDOM

LIFE'S GREAT TREASURE

RICHARD E. SIMMONS III

Union Hill Publishing

Wisdom Life's Great Treasure

Union Hill Publishing
200 Union Hill Drive, Suite 200
Birmingham, AL 35209

www.thecenterbham.org

ISBN 978-1- 939358-13- 4

1 2 3 4 5 6 7 8 9 10

Printed in the United States of America

To my three wonderful children,
Dixon, Pate and Will;
May you walk in wisdom all the days of your life.

Table of Contents

TABLE OF CONTENTS

Introduction

FOR THE LAST 50 years, I have been intrigued by the concept of "wisdom." As a young boy I remember hearing these words from Solomon about wisdom, "She is more precious than jewels and nothing you desire compares with her." (Proverbs 3:15) The fact that nothing in this life compares with wisdom grabbed my attention, therefore, I have been on a lifelong search to understand and to acquire it. My children will tell you that one of the great desires I have for them is that they become people of great wisdom.

Several years ago, I read an enlightening excerpt from the great roman philosopher and statesman, Seneca. He was born in 4 B.C., and wrote about wisdom in one of his famous essays, "On the Happy Life." He noted that too many people wander aimlessly through life, never looking for guidance. They follow only the noise and contradictions of those who seek to have us follow them. Seneca concludes that this is what leads us into a host of problems and mistakes. And since this life is so brief, we should strive day and night for sound wisdom.

Seneca then added, "Nothing, therefore, needs to be more emphasized than the warning that we should not, like sheep, follow the lead of the throng in front of us, traveling, thus, the way that all go and not the way we ought to go."

Wisdom begins with a true interpretation of the world and how we should live in it. To lack wisdom is to be without direction and to be lost in a world that does not make sense. Scholar Neal Plantinga reveals that the correct order of life is wisdom. He then gives a great definition, stating that wisdom is "finding out the truth about what life is, what makes the world work and how we ought to fit into it."

This explains why wisdom is of such abundant value. It not only gives coherence to life, but also provides a path leading to our ultimate well-being and happiness. We should all stop and ask, "What is that worth to me?"

This book is a collection of short essays on wisdom. They come from all my reading, research, teaching and writing over the past 40 years. I take 12 of the most strategic issues in life, and provide four or five short essays (they can be read in five to seven minutes) on each issue listed below:

The Nature of Wisdom
Personal Growth and Development
Wisdom and True Freedom
Wisdom in the Search for Meaning
Business and Career Wisdom
Financial Wisdom
Relational Wisdom
Human Sexuality
Care of the Soul
Wisdom and a Healthy Life
The Storms of Life
Facing Our Mortality

The book closes with a chapter on what I consider to be five of the most important principles that govern life.

My hope is that this book serves as a guide to help you walk in wisdom on your journey toward a healthy and meaningful life.

THE NATURE OF
WISDOM

Make wisdom your provision for the journey from youth to old age,
for it is a more certain support than all other possessions.

--Bias of Priene

The Path
of Wisdom

IN ALL OF my research and studies throughout my career, I have been fascinated by the writings of many educators and thinkers, including those of Dr. Richard Light, the Carl H. Pforzheimer Professor of Teaching at Harvard Graduate School of Education. He wrote an article that appeared in a 2015 issue of *The New York Times* titled, "How to Live Wisely," opening with an enlightening passage:

> *Imagine you are dean for a day. What is one actionable change you would implement to enhance the college experience on campus?*
>
> *I have asked students this question for years. The answers can be eye-opening. A few years ago, the responses began to move away from "tweak the history course" or "change the ways labs are structured." A different commentary, about learning to live wisely, has emerged.*

Reflecting on his words, it seems modern life is not working for these young people and they have no idea why. They recognize that they are not living wisely. Instead, we are following the present-day dictates of our culture, breaking down life in return.

I am hopeful that more individuals like these students are waking up to realize how important it is to learn how to live wisely, especially since wisdom is one of the greatest of all of life's possessions. Yet, before we can do that, it's important to understand the basic meaning of wisdom.

The word "wisdom" comes from the Hebrew word *chokmah* that literally translates to have "skill or expertise in living." This essential component of wisdom gives one the ability to see things as they really are and not just as they appear to be. This ability is vital to the foundation of wisdom, because we continually develop ideas explaining how our lives work as we move through various seasons of life. These ideas govern our thinking, designating what the world is like and how we are to live in it.

Wisdom enables us to distinguish between those ideas in life that are true and those that are false.

Author Stephen Covey contends that if people are truly going to lead healthy, vibrant lives, their ideas about life must be rooted in what is true. He shares a wonderful illustration, demonstrating the importance of this truth:

Suppose you wanted to arrive at a specific location in central Chicago. A street map of the city would be a great help to you in reaching your destination. But suppose you were given the wrong map. Through a printing error, the map labeled "Chicago" was actually a map of Detroit. Can you imagine the frustration, the ineffectiveness of trying to reach your destination?

You might work on your behavior—you could try harder, be more diligent, double your speed. But your efforts would only succeed in getting you to the wrong place faster.

You might work on your attitude—you could think more positively. You still wouldn't get to the right place, but perhaps you wouldn't care. Your attitude would be so positive, you'd be happy wherever you were.

The point is, you'd still be lost. The fundamental problem has nothing to do with your behavior or your attitude. It has everything to do with having the wrong map.

If you have the right map of Chicago, then diligence becomes important, and when you encounter frustrating obstacles along the way, then attitude can make a real difference. But the first and most important requirement is the accuracy of the map.

I find this to be true in the lives of so many people. They attempt to live their lives with maps that are entirely inaccurate. They have false ideas about life, money, work, success, identity and happiness. What they do not realize is they interpret everything through these false maps—false ideas—that have mentally developed over the course of their lives.

Expanding on this notion, French mathematician and philosopher Blaise Pascal, considered by many to be one of the most brilliant men to ever live, recognized something extraordinary. All human beings are on a great search for happiness, but most find it to be elusive. He strongly believed that unhappiness is a result of false beliefs on matters important for living a high quality of life. He contends that true happiness can only be found by uprooting false beliefs and replacing them with genuine wisdom.

The Age of Information Overload

We live in a time where we are flooded with information. Many people are convinced they have a real advantage in life when they have a great deal of knowledge. Yet, every day we read of highly educated fools who ruin their lives, businesses and families by making bad decisions. Often, it's knowledgeable people who lack wisdom.

We fail to recognize that the *quantity* of what we know is not of ultimate importance. What matters is the *quality* of our knowledge, which is at the heart of wisdom.

Further supporting this view, author Richard Foster shares that superficiality is the curse of the modern age. He contends that our desperate need is not for a greater number of intelligent or gifted people, but for a greater number of wise people who have gained depth in their lives. He believes wisdom is the answer to a hollow world.

Unfortunately, much of today's society dismisses the nature and value of wisdom to the point where it is no longer of real importance. For most of us, the distractions and frantic pace of a technology-driven culture do not encourage deep thought, reflection or introspection.

Furthermore, much of the population feels the ultimate outcome of their lives depends on the moral choices they make. If they make good moral choices, then life is good. And certainly, bad moral choices can destroy one's life. But, this is only partially true. Wisdom deals with true clarity in our thinking, and this is why we treasure it. It is much more than just being moral and good.

Wisdom is knowing what to do, and not just in moral situations. As a matter of fact, wisdom applies in the vast majority of life's situations, where moral rules have only nominal application. The first time I read this thought, developed by author Tim Keller, I was grateful for his remarkable gift of insight. He contends that most of the choices and decisions we make are not specifically moral choices.

For example, the following are some of the pivotal but not essentially moral driven issues in our lives:

- Career choice or change
- Marriage choice
- Dealing with your teenager
- Financial decisions
- Investment decisions

Questions we may ask include:

- Should I confront someone? What should I say?
- Should I take this risk?
- How should I spend my time?
- What are my priorities?

Wisdom provides insight into the true nature of reality—both physical and spiritual. It allows us to grow in competence as we respond to the realities of life. Wisdom is knowing how things truly work and why things happen, and then knowing what to do about it.

God's Design for Life

It is imperative to recognize that there is a pattern or fabric in all reality. Life is governed by certain laws and principles. They are not "good", "bad", "moral" or "immoral," they are simply true. What is crucial for us to grasp is that these principles actually make life predictable. Such an understanding creates the potential for certain outcomes in our lives. Most significantly, our lives will flourish when they are in harmony with these principles.

Covey puts it like this:

Principles always have natural consequences attached to them. There are positive consequences when we live in harmony with the principles. There are negative consequences when we ignore them. But because these principles apply to everyone, whether or not they are aware, this limitation is universal. And the more we know of correct principles, the greater is our ability to live wisely. By centering our lives on timeless, unchanging principles, we create a fundamental paradigm of effective living.

Covey is clear that you cannot violate these fundamental principles with impunity. Whether we believe in them or not, these unchanging principles have proven to be valid throughout all of human history.

1.2

The Value
of Wisdom

HAVE YOU EVER seen a person live recklessly on the edge until, one day, he or she crashes into the wall of reality? Unfortunately, that person did not have the protection of wisdom.

Wisdom allows us to understand the laws and principles of life, enabling us to harmonize our lives with reality. So, instead of running headlong into reality, we prosper in our relationship with it. Ultimately, wisdom protects us.

Years ago, I read a simple illustration that provides great insight into the way wisdom works in our lives.

A little girl watches her mother ironing clothes. The child is intrigued by the process as the iron eats up the wrinkles and creases in each garment. The phone rings. As the mother goes to answer it, she says to her little girl, "Don't touch that iron; it's hot." The child now has knowledge—the iron is hot. As soon as her mother disappears, the little girl decides to try her own hand at ironing. Unfortunately she touches the iron in the wrong place and is burned. She now has understanding—the iron is hot. The next day the mother continues with the ironing and again she is summoned by the phone. Once again, she issues a warning: "Don't touch the iron; it's hot." The temptation to iron clothes comes over the little girl. She puts out her hand to grab the iron. Then she remembers her burned finger and leaves the iron alone. She now has wisdom—the iron is hot.

From this simplistic story, we see how wisdom impacts the decisions and choices we make. When you get right down to it, wisdom changes people. It impacts not only what you see, but also the choices and decisions you make. At the end of the day, it is your choices that determine the ultimate outcome of your life.

It strikes me that wise people are very forward thinking. They understand that all of life is connected. There is a cause and effect relationship between the choices one makes today, and what one experiences tomorrow.

In Proverbs 27:12, Solomon says:

"A prudent man sees evil and hides himself, the naïve proceed and pay the penalty."

In commenting on this verse, author Andy Stanley says:

Prudent people look as far down the road as possible when making decisions. Every decision. After all, they understand that today and tomorrow are connected. As the author of Proverbs states, they stay on the lookout for signs of trouble up ahead. Today's decisions are informed and influenced by their impact on tomorrow. Drawing on their own experience and the experience of others, they anticipate the future and choose accordingly. They ask, "In light of my past experience and my future hopes and dreams, what's the wise thing to do?" The prudent draw upon the wealth of data that life has already provided them and take appropriate action when they see danger ahead.

In contrast to the prudent, the simple or naïve person lives as though life is disconnected; as if there is no connection between today's choices and tomorrow's experiences. When the simple "see danger," they don't take evasive action. They keep going.

Notice, I said they live as if life is disconnected. They don't necessarily believe that to be the case. If you were to ask them, "Do you think there is a connection between the choices you make today and what you will experience in the future?" they would probably answer, "Yes." Again, it is not that they don't believe life is connected. The point is they don't live as if it is.

Take for example the 1960s. It was a turbulent time in our country when young people did not like the structure they witnessed in the lives of their parents. They desired to be liberated from the restrictions that the culture imposed upon them. Many of them dropped out of mainstream society and lived in communes.

It was later in the decade that a group of hippies living in the Haight-Ashbury District of San Francisco decided that hygiene was a middle class hang-up they could do without. Though baths and showers, while not actually banned, were frowned upon. The novelist Tom Wolfe was intrigued by these hippies, who he said "sought nothing less than to sweep aside all codes and restraints of the past and start out from zero." They aspired to be totally autonomous and free.

Before long, the hippies' aversion to modern hygiene had consequences that were as unpleasant as they were unforeseen. Wolfe gives this description:

At the Haight-Ashbury Free Clinic, there were doctors who were treating diseases no living doctor had ever encountered before, diseases that had disappeared so long ago that they had never even picked up Latin names, such as the mange, the grunge, the scroff and the rot.

The itching and the mange began to vex these hippies, leading them to seek help from the local free clinics. Step by step, they were forced to rediscover for themselves the necessity of modern hygiene.

Clearly, all of life has an underlying design and structure. We have certain universal principles that are built into life, and we violate them at our own risk.

Wisdom recognizes the importance of honoring this underlying structure. This is why Solomon says, "Wisdom preserves the lives of its possessors." (Ecclesiastes 7:12).

1.3

Wisdom and the Pursuit of Happiness

W HAT DO YOU want most out of life? If you were to conduct street interviews in any city and ask this question, the answer you would overwhelmingly hear is "happiness." It seems to be the universal response in all places, at all times.

Going back to the early Greek philosophers, a group of men in search of wisdom journeyed to discover how individuals could live a good and happy life. Aristotle called happiness "the highest good," reflecting that an enlightened society would be ordered with the goal of helping its citizens become happy. The problem is, the Greeks could never land on a unified answer of how to find it.

Also on a quest for the root of happiness, French philosopher Blaise Pascal addressed these words in his 1660 classic book, *Pensées*:

> All men seek happiness. There are no exceptions. However different the means they may employ, they all strive toward this goal!

However, Pascal saw nothing but unhappiness all around him. He said, "as unhappy as we are . . . we have an idea of happiness but we cannot obtain it." He went on to conclude that instead of being happy, we struggle with "inconstancy, boredom and anxiety."

Fast forward to 1930 when Sigmund Freud published his book, *Civilization and Its Discontent*. Freud originally planned to title it *Un-*

happiness in Civilization, but was convinced otherwise. The book's central theme is the frustration one experiences in the perennial search for happiness. Freud recognized this as the driving force of all people. He perceived our desire for happiness to be insatiable. However, what most people don't know is that happiness eluded Freud his entire life. In fact, he referred to life as being joyless and full of misery.

Happiness and the Social Sciences

Over the last 20 years, social scientists have performed research at the University of Chicago, Princeton, Harvard and Yale to better understand personal happiness and its relationship with rising prosperity. The results were baffling. Researchers learned that, as prosperity rises in the western world, our sense of well-being does not move toward happiness; rather, it retreats.

Princeton professor Dr. Daniel Kahneman, who won a Nobel Prize for Economics in 2002, spent two decades observing the "subjective well-being"—a common phrase social scientists use to describe happiness—in people's lives, and eventually abandoned his work. During this 20-year period, Dr. Kahneman was unable to summarize conclusive insights regarding a person's happiness.

Gregg Easterbrook is a popular journalist and a contributing editor at *The New Republic* and *The Atlantic Monthly*. His 2003 book, *The Progress Paradox: How Life Gets Better While People Feel Worse*, asserts that almost all aspects of western civilization have vastly improved in the last 100 years, while men and women of today are not as happy as in previous generations. Easterbrook makes this observation:

> How many of us feel positive about our moment, or even believe that life is getting better? Today, Americans tell pollsters that the country is going downhill; that their parents had it better; that they feel unbearably stressed out; that their children face a declining future—and Americans were telling pollsters this even during the unprecedented boom that preceded the tragedy of September 11, 2001.
>
> Far from feeling better about their lives, many are feeling

worse. Throughout the United States and the European Union, incidence of clinical melancholy has been rising in eerie synchronization with rising prosperity: adjusting for population growth, "unipolar" depression, the condition in which a person simply always feels blue, is today ten times as prevalent as it was half a century ago.

There is increasing evidence from other sources to support Easterbrook's claim.

In their 2003 book, *Healing Anxiety and Depression,* Dr. Daniel Amen and Dr. Lisa Routh claim, "Anxiety and depression are major public health problems reaching epidemic levels in the United States."

Dr. Martin Seligman, a psychologist who teaches at the University of Pennsylvania and author of the bestselling book, *Flourish: A Visionary New Understanding of Happiness and Wellbeing,* has spent his entire career studying human happiness. Dr. Seligman highlights in his research that the baby boomer generation has experienced a significant increase in depression compared to earlier generations. This rise can only lead to one conclusion–an epidemic in modern culture, which explains the explosion of our suicide rate.

Joining the quest for the source of happiness, philosopher Deal Hudson presented his argument on psychological happiness:

[Psychological happiness] has become an unquestioned first principle of the present age. As a result, the cultivation of satisfaction, pleasure and emotion now takes precedence over the nurturing of moral and institutional character.

We have gone from a time when self-restraint was a cardinal virtue, to one where self-gratification is the driving force in people's lives.

Finding the Right Path

Although these findings appear grim, the purpose of this book is to help people understand why they are coming up short in their pursuit of happiness. It is indeed a great paradox. We live in such prosperity, in a country where we are free to pursue our dreams. Yet, disappointment and despair surround us as we continue down the wrong path. Perhaps it is time to be open to the possibility that our ideas about happiness may, in fact, be wrong.

Dr. Seligman provides great insight into what has happened. He suggests we no longer live as our ancestors, who lived for a cause much bigger than themselves: God, family, country. In the past, people tied happiness to the right ordering of the soul. It was considered a reward for living wisely.

C. S. Lewis makes a shrewd observation about living wisely in his book, *The Abolition of Man*. He states that ancient wisdom recognized that man's chief problem was how to conform his or her soul to reality. The answer to this is by acquiring wisdom. In other words, wisdom is the answer to the cardinal problem of life. Lewis says, "Here is life, and I need to see and understand how it works, and then seek to live in harmony with it." This is wisdom. This is what leads to our ultimate well-being.

1.4

Wisdom: The Key to a Healthy Life

I F YOU EXAMINE our culture closely you cannot help but notice that modern people are not very healthy. There is extraordinary dysfunction, and many adults, teenagers and children struggle to cope with life.

When I speak of being healthy, I am referring to our mental, emotional, psychological and spiritual well-being. We seem to have lost our way and I contend that our lack of healthiness is what is causing people to be so unhappy. The bottom line is unhealthy people are unhappy people.

Dr. Scott Peck gives great insight into this issue in his bestselling book, *The Road Less Traveled*. His opening words in the book are, "Life is difficult." Dr. Peck proceeds to explain how life is a series of problems. We can complain and ignore our problems, or we can seek to solve them. Confronting and dealing with problems can be painful. However, Dr. Peck believes the process of facing and solving problems is key to achieving mental and spiritual health. He then shares what is key in becoming a healthy person. Dr. Peck calls it "being dedicated to the truth."

He says:

The more clearly we see the reality of the world, the better equipped we are to deal with the world. The less clearly we see the reality of the world—the more our minds are befuddled by

falsehood, misperceptions and illusions—the less able we will be
to determine correct courses of action and make wise decisions.

Like Stephen Covey, Peck believes our view of reality is like a map,
negotiating the terrain of life. He says:

> If the map is true and accurate, we will generally know where
> we are, and if we have decided where we want to go, we will
> generally know how to get there. If the map is false and inaccu-
> rate, we generally will be lost.

If we are committed to the truth, it is like an accurate map for our
lives. This map tells us:

Where we are.
Where we need to go.
How to get there.

On the other hand, if a person does not have the right map, he or she
will be lost, finding life to be very difficult and incoherent.

Truth, however painful it might be, is our friend, leading to our
well-being. True wisdom is to discern the truth and seek to live in accordance with it.

Philosopher Dr. George Graham made this interesting observation:

> It takes a tremendous amount of courage to face the truth. Peo-
> ple who have the habit of not facing the truth have a habit of
> having trouble living in every aspect of their lives—in their jobs,
> in their personal relationships . . . being centered on the truth is
> critical to a healthy, vital, human life.

When I speak of the importance of facing the truth, I am talking about
confronting the truth about ourselves and our circumstances. We generally like the truth until it begins to lead us in a direction we do not
want to go.

So I would ask you to look at your life and do your own evaluation.

Ask yourself:

- Am I a (mentally, emotionally and spiritually) healthy person?
- Are my relationships healthy?
- Do I have serious flaws that remain hidden from everyone else?
- What about destructive habits in my life?
- Is my work suffocating or consuming me?
- Am I growing and developing as a person?
- Do I have problems that I am afraid of and refuse to deal with?
- What is the state of my spiritual life?

In the New Testament, John, chapter five, Jesus encounters a crippled man and asks the man an unusual question:

Do you want to get well?

This is a question we all should ask ourselves. *Do I want to get well? Do I want to be healthy?* Unfortunately, many delude themselves into believing that everything will eventually work out and end up doing nothing.

To me, it is clear that wise people love the truth. They recognize that truth is their friend.

PERSONAL GROWTH
AND DEVELOPMENT

Without continual growth and progress, such words as
improvement, achievement and success have no meaning.
--Benjamin Franklin

A Life That Flourishes

D R. GERALD BELL currently teaches at the University of North Carolina Kenan-Flagler Business School. He conducted an interesting study interviewing business executives who had just retired from successful business careers. Each of them was asked, "If you could relive your career, what would you have done differently?"

Responses varied, but the number one reply was, "I should have taken charge of my life and set my goals and objectives earlier."

One of the greatest truths I have learned is that if you are serious about individual growth and development, you have to be intentional about it. You must endeavor to plan for growth or it will never happen. This applies to every aspect of life.

Most people cannot grasp this, and the study explains why there is such a gap between the life we dream of and aspire to, and the life we actually end up living. For most of us, this is a reality.

In the books of Psalms and Proverbs, we are told that each of us are on a certain path, leading in a specific direction. We are instructed to go down a path that leads to wisdom and understanding, eventually reaching a sense of well-being and a life of excellence.

In his book, *The Principle of the Path*, Andy Stanley writes that everyone is on a path at this moment, whether we realize it or not. This path takes each of us to a certain destination. It is not a respecter of person; it does not care who you are or where you are from. It leads where it leads regardless of your talent, wealth, physical appearance or social status.

When you meet someone who is leading an extraordinary life, how do you think it has come to pass? Do you believe it was an accident or a stroke of good fortune? What we know is that people are where they are in their life as a result of decisions, which have formed the path leading to their present circumstances.

Think about the various paths you are going down. For example, you are currently on a physical health path and it is taking you in a certain direction. This path will impact the length of your life and the quality of your life as you age.

Likewise, your marriage is on a specific path. It will determine the quality of the relationship you will experience with your spouse as the years go by. If you have children at home, you are on a child-rearing path that will determine the type of adults your children will become. We are each on a financial path, a moral path, an intellectual path, a career path and a spiritual path. These paths always determine our end results.

I have concluded that one of the primary reasons we have great discrepancies between what we desire in our hearts and what we end up doing with our lives is because we live with great intentions. We have been deceived into thinking that great intentions will take us where we want to go in life.

Clayton Christensen, a Rhodes scholar and professor at Harvard Business School, wrote this in the July 2010 Harvard Business Review:

Over the years I have watched the fates of my Harvard Business School classmates from 1979 unfold. I have seen more and more of them come to reunions unhappy, divorced and alienated from their children. I can guarantee that not a single one of them graduated with the deliberate strategy of getting divorced and raising children who would be estranged from them.

Yet, they went down a path that led to this consequence.

All couples enter into marriage with great intentions for their future together, but without realizing it, a number of them choose a path that leads to divorce.

We all have good intentions for our lives, but at the end of the day, it is the direction of the path, not good intentions, that, ultimately, determines our destination in life.

It is crucial that we examine these important areas of our lives— God, marriage, children, health and finances, create a plan for growth, and then execute that plan.

As I've mentioned, if you want to grow and develop any area of your life, *you have to be intentional. You must plan for growth, or it will never happen.*

2.2

The Art of
Achieving

I RECENTLY READ an interesting book, *Flourish*, written by prominent psychologist Dr. Martin Seligman, who teaches at the University of Pennsylvania.

In his book, Dr. Seligman notes the basic equation to growth, development and achievement in any area of life is based on the skill and ability you have, multiplied by the effort you expend. He defines effort as the time you are willing to spend on a task.

Dr. Seligman looks to the findings of Dr. Anders Ericsson, a professor of psychology at Florida State University.

Dr. Ericsson argues that the cornerstone of all high expertise is not God-given genius but deliberate practice: Mozart was Mozart, not primarily because he had a unique gift for music, but because he spent all of his time using his gift since his toddlerhood. World-class chess players are not faster of thought, nor do they have unusually good memories for moves. Rather, they have so much experience that they are vastly better at recognizing patterns in chess positions than novice chess players, and this comes from sheer experience.

Dr. Seligman makes an interesting observation about the time we are willing to devote to growth and achievement. He says it has to do with our character. Self-discipline, the trait that engenders deliberate practice, is defined as the ability to make yourself do something you don't necessarily want to do, to get a result you would like to have.

He also shares interesting research on self-discipline with the students of Mastermind High School in Philadelphia. Mastermind accepts promising students beginning in the fifth grade, although numerous students wash out even before the real competition begins in the ninth grade. The researchers studied a group of the school's eighth graders to find out how self-discipline compares with IQ in predicting academic achievement.

They employed a battery of tests to determine which students possessed the character trait of self-discipline. For instance, they looked at how well the students could delay gratification. They might have asked, "Would you rather I give you five dollars today or ten dollars in two weeks?"

They then studied the highly self-disciplined eighth graders and they found that these students:

- Reflected higher grade point averages
- Earned higher achievement test scores
- Spent more time on homework, started it earlier in the day
- Showed lower absenteeism
- Watched less television

In the end, their research concluded that self-discipline out-predicts IQ for academic success by a factor of about two.

From my research, I have observed that when we underachieve in any area of life, we often look for something or someone to blame. In reality, the real reason is because of an unwillingness to sacrifice short-term pleasure for long-term gain.

Dr. Seligman believes his findings apply to every area of our lives. Although I agree, I contend there is another vital component to all of this involving affections of the heart. That is, we invest our time in what our hearts treasure. As Jesus Himself put it; "For wherever your treasure and riches lie, there will your heart be also." (Mathew 6:21)

In reflection, I leave you with this question: What do you treasure most in your life? Your answer will determine where your heart is and how you will discipline your life.

2.3

Priorities

I FIRST READ the illustration below in best-selling author Stephen Covey's book, *First Things First*. It is undeniably powerful as it pertains to the priorities of life:

One day this expert was speaking to a group of business students and, to drive home a point, used an illustration I'm sure those students will never forget.

As this man stood in front of the group of high-powered overachievers, he said, "Okay, time for a quiz." Then he pulled out a one-gallon, wide-mouthed Mason jar and set it on a table in front of him. Then he produced about a dozen fist-sized rocks and carefully placed them, one at a time, into the jar.

When the jar was filled to the top and no more rocks would fit inside, he asked, "Is this jar full?" Everyone in the class said, "Yes." Then he said, "Really?" He reached under the table and pulled out a bucket of gravel. Then he dumped some of the gravel in and shook the jar, causing pieces of gravel to work themselves down into the spaces between the big rocks.

Then he smiled and asked the group once more, "Is the jar full?" By this time the class was onto him. "Probably not," one of them answered. "Good!" he replied. And he reached under the table and brought out a bucket of sand. He started dumping the sand in and it went into all the spaces left between the rocks and the gravel. Once more he asked the question, "Is this jar full?"

"No!" the class shouted. Once again he said, "Good!" Then he grabbed a pitcher of water and began to pour it in until the jar was filled to the brim. He looked up at the class and asked, "What is the point of this illustration?"

One eager beaver raised his hand and said, "The point is, no matter how full your schedule is, if you try really hard, you can always fit some more things into it!"

"No," the speaker replied, "that's not the point. The truth this illustration teaches us is: If you don't put the big rocks in first, you'll never get them in at all."

The jar is your life. The big rocks are the things that matter most in life, beginning with your relationship with God, your marriage and other important relationships.

The small pebbles are important but not nearly as important as the big rocks. This would include your job, exercise, finances and reading.

The sand and the water are things in life we enjoy, but are not important in the grand scheme of things. In fact, they are often viewed as trivial.

Plenty of people are convinced that to experience a full and happy life, you need to fill the jar with as much as you can. In reality, the jar—your life—can only hold so much.

If you are serious about living wisely, getting the most out of life, you have to prioritize correctly. Put the big rocks in first. Most people cannot grasp this notion. They let the gravel, sand and water become more important than the big rocks.

Unfortunately, we live in a culture that greatly values the trivial pursuits of life—sand and water—and we easily get carried away by culture's priorities. This is why you must decide in advance, "What comes first in my life?"

2.4

Disordered Priorities

I RECENTLY READ an interview with Dr. Armond Nicholi, the editor of *The Harvard Guide to Psychiatry*. He also teaches at the undergraduate college and at Harvard Medical School. Dr. Nicholi is a gifted lecturer and maintains an active clinical practice in psychiatry.

In his interview, Nicholi reveals:

> I teach people who are just starting out. As Harvard students, they're all bright to start with, and they often have talents or interests that they're actively pursuing. But, early in the semester I ask them, "What is your goal in life?" Invariably they answer, "To be successful." So I ask, "What does that mean to you?" Their answer has some relationship to fame and fortune.

But, then he offers the students another framework.

"I tell them we all have a lifespan of about 30,000 days," Dr. Nicholi says, "and we spend about a third of that time sleeping. That means we have a waking lifespan of about 20,000 days. Then I say, 'If you had 20 days left, what would you do with them?' They universally answer that they would spend that time working on their relationships with family and friends, and if they're people of faith, with their God."

He lets that soak in for a few days, and then in a subsequent lecture, Dr. Nicholi suggests to the students that "fame and fortune," which they claim to want more than anything, are actually in conflict with their highest stated priority of friends and family. They become so intensely focused on what they want to achieve through wealth and glory that they largely neglect the things they value most in life—their relationships.

Dr. Nicholi goes on to illustrate that most of these students, nevertheless, forge ahead in their pursuit of fame and fortune. They end up with spouses who are of secondary importance to them, and they do not have a close relationship with their children. They end up with what Dr. Nicholi calls "disordered priorities."

I am amazed at how our desire for fame, wealth and glory can blind us to what really matters in life. C. S. Lewis clearly observed this and warned his students in a renowned speech, "The Inner Ring," he delivered at Kings College at the University of London.

As Lewis addressed the students, he warned them of the natural human desire to always want to be a part of the correct inner circles. He explained that these inner circles, these cliques, will inevitably form and reform, in constant change throughout the seasons of a person's life. They provide no real stability.

He cautioned these students about the consuming ambition to be an insider, cozying up to those who are important and well-to-do to be part of an imagined elite. In doing so, Lewis says we become like the weary traveler in the desert who chases a mirage. Ultimately, our quest to be in the inner circle of the powerful will one day break our hearts.

This is the choice we all face. We can continue to allow this world to define who we are and what our lives are worth, with the knowledge that one day the world will invariably break our hearts. Or, we can break the world's hold on our lives by relinquishing ourselves and our identities to become absolutely grounded in Christ's love and His commitment to our well-being. Make no mistake; irrespective of our station in life, it is a choice we all have to make that will make or break us as men and women.

2.5

A Plan for Growth

I GAINED GREAT insight when I read of a conversation author John Maxwell had 40 years ago that radically changed his life. He was enjoying breakfast with Curt Kampmeier, a business executive coach, at a Holiday Inn in Lancaster, Ohio, when Kampmeier posed this thought-provoking question:

"John, what is your plan for personal growth?"

Never at a loss for words, I searched for factors in my life that might qualify for growth. I told him about the various activities I was engaged in throughout the week. And I spoke about how hard I worked and my achievements within my organization. I must have talked for 10 minutes, until I finally ran out of gas. Curt listened patiently, smiled and finally asked, "You don't have a personal plan for growth, do you?"

"No," I reluctantly admitted.

"You know," Curt said simply, "growth is not an automatic process."

Maxwell realized that, to grow, you have to have a plan for growth.

Noted business consultant and author Stephen Covey takes a slightly varied approach in confronting this same issue by posing a series of questions. What is the one activity that you **know** if you did superbly well and consistently, would have significant results in your personal life? What is the one activity that you **know** if you did superbly well and consistently would have significant results in your professional or work life? If you **know** these things would make such a significant difference, why are you not doing them right now?

Covey concludes there is one primary reason we seldom pursue these activities: we do not consider them with any real sense of urgency. We recognize they are important, but not pressing. Therefore, we procrastinate with the justification, "I will get to it eventually."

I am not certain we fully comprehend that the important activities of life do not act on us often; we must make clear and conscious choices to act on them. This lack of awareness is perhaps why we spend our lives reacting to the urgent demands of life, and then wonder why we see no growth or improvement in the most strategic areas of our lives. As a result, in our day-to-day decision-making, the "urgent" seems to dominate over the "important," which causes us to experience little personal growth, and at best, a mediocre life.

Several years ago, I encountered a principle regarding personal growth that has powerfully impacted my own life. It is called the "Vector Principle," and I first read about it in Jerry Foster's book, *Life Focus.*

Vector, a term in mathematics and physics, quantifies the speed and direction of an object. If you were the pilot of a jetliner, you would use vectors to define the course to your destination. When you are given a new vector by the control center, you turn the plane to line up with that heading on the compass, creating a new vector angle.

Obviously, even the smallest vector change in the cockpit can make a vast difference in the plane's ultimate destination. Though it may seem an imperceptible change, with every mile you are farther from your previous course. For example, upon leaving New York, you could make a tiny vector change while flying to Seattle, landing in Los Angeles instead.

The Vector Principle applies to our lives in the same manner. Even if you never fly an airplane, you are vectoring through life by the choices you make. You are currently on a course that was determined by choices you made since you were aware of your capacity to choose. Many of these choices looked fairly insignificant at the time, but small changes make a big difference over time.

This is significant. **Small changes make a big difference with the passage of time.** You may not realize it, but the most significant achievements in life are the result of many little things done in a single, strategic direction.

Therefore, at the beginning of each year, I choose to make three or four small, relevant changes in the most important areas of my life. After 30 or 40 days, they become habits. And these habits create a ripple effect as the years go by.

I read recently where Pat Williams, former NBA coach and current senior vice-president of the Orlando Magic, was having dinner with the legendary basketball coach, John Wooden. At one point during the meal, Williams asked Coach Wooden, "Coach, if you could pinpoint just one secret of success in life, what would it be?"

Coach Wooden considered his response for a minute and confidently replied, "The closest I can come to one single secret of success is this: a lot of little things done well."

2.6

The Power of
a Focused Life

IRECENTLY READ an interview in the *Harvard Business Review* with Hewlett Packard CEO Meg Whitman on why she had split the company, forming two separate corporations. She is now the CEO of Hewlett Packard Enterprises, focusing on software and business services, while Dion Weisler is the CEO of HP Inc., which sells hardware. When Whitman was asked how this new arrangement was working for the companies, she responded:

> The separation will be judged a success if the two companies go on to thrive as industry leaders. Already I can see a difference in how they're run. Dion Weisler, HP Inc.'s CEO, is focused on his business; I'm focused on mine. I had underestimated the benefit of focus, because you can't put it in a cash flow model. It's a remarkable accelerant.

She makes a great point. There is a power when you focus your life and have fewer distractions. In one sense, you become much more effective by being increasingly selective in how you spend your time.

In his best-selling book, *The Purpose Driven Life*, Rick Warren addresses the power of a focused life:

> *The power of focusing can be seen in light. Diffused light has little power or impact, but you can concentrate its energy by focusing it.*

With a magnifying glass, the rays of the sun can be focused to set grass or paper on fire. When light is focused even more as a laser beam, it can cut through steel.

There is nothing quite as potent as a focused life, one lived on purpose. The men and women who have made the greatest differences in history were the most focused.

I find that in this modern world, our lives are scattered, going in too many directions. We become easily distracted from what matters most. This is particularly true when it comes to our spiritual lives.

I am reminded of an incident in the Bible in the book of Luke, where Jesus is in the home of Martha and Mary. Luke describes it in the tenth chapter, verses 38–42.

Now as they were traveling along, He entered a village, and a woman named Martha welcomed Him into her home. She had a sister called Mary who was seated at the Lord's feet, listening to His word.

But, Martha was distracted with all her preparations, and she came up to Him and said, 'Lord, do You not care that my sister has left me to do all the serving alone? Then tell her to help me.' But, the Lord answered and said to her, 'Martha, Martha, you are worried and bothered about so many things, but only one thing is necessary, for Mary has chosen the good part, which shall not be taken away from her.'

Notice the words that were used to describe Martha: "distracted, worried and bothered." Does that ever describe your life? Notice that Jesus' response to her has nothing to do with right or wrong. It is not a moral issue that He raises with Martha. It is a priority issue. Jesus is revealing that, as humans, we get too busy, distracted and worried about trivial issues in life. Only a few things truly matter, and there is one thing that should be our highest priority, more important than everything else. Jesus points to Mary as an example. We see in verse 39, "she was seated at the Lord's feet, listening to His word."

Jesus makes it clear that only a few things in life have great value, but so many of us are like Martha, moving in countless directions, drawn away from what matters most. In the end, I believe we are required to simplify our lives so we are less likely to be diverted by the things of life that are ultimately of little importance.

Several years ago, Bob and Judy Fisher, a husband-and-wife team living in Nashville, Tennessee, wrote an interesting book titled *Life Is a Gift*. It focuses on, among other things, a life of regret. The Fishers interviewed 104 terminally ill patients, all of them under hospice care. In each case, a recurring theme appeared:

So many people realized too late that there was a significant gap between the things they ought to be doing in their lives and the things they actually did.

Sadly, this is what happens. We fritter away our lives because we refuse to focus on what really matters. We unknowingly create a huge gap between the life we dream of and aspire to, and the life we end up with.

I cannot be more emphatic: *There is power in a focused life!*

WISDOM AND TRUE FREEDOM

*Freedom without wisdom or responsibility is the
greatest of all possible evils.*
~ Edmund Burke

3.1

Freedom and the Control of Our Desires

W HEN YOU FOCUS on what matters most in your life, do you think about freedom? What is freedom to you?

The great Oxford philosopher Isaiah Berlin was known to share with his students that there are two types of freedom—negative and positive. In today's modern world, many individuals view freedom in negative terms such as *freedom from* restrictions or *freedom from* restraints. These restraints hinder us from fulfilling our hearts' greatest desires. Negative freedom says, *I am only free from outside influence to do what my heart desires.*

On the flip side, Berlin deems freedom in the positive form to be *freedom for,* in essence, *freedom for* excellence to be all that you were meant to be. To a musician, a dancer or an athlete, positive freedom involves self-control, training and discipline instead of negative freedom's self-indulgence.

Author and social critic Os Guinness imparts that Winston Churchill would often quote Alexander the Great, who touted that the Persians would always be slaves because they could never say "no." He states that true freedom thrives on self-restraint and the power to say "no." A culture that cannot curb its desires is a culture with no future.

Guinness reveals that freedom requires a clear refusal of what is false, bad, excessive and destructive. As a result, we need to aspire to virtue, justice, excellence and beauty. We should not just understand these ideals, we should purposefully live them out, allowing them to become part of the foundation of who we really are.

There are Americans today who think no one should surrender his or her spiritual or moral authority to anyone. Not even to God. Particularly God. We have come to believe that, if you surrender your life to God and obey Him, He will abuse you; He will steal your happiness from you.

But, you have to wonder, why would the God who made us and loves us want to make us unhappy? Have you ever thought that possibly God has designed the ultimate path to happiness? In reality, we do not like the path or do not believe it will deliver freedom. Instead, we believe God will consistently cross our wills and deprive us of our freedom. Even so, there are times our wills are in great need of being crossed for our ultimate good and well-being.

Let's assume you decide to get serious about getting your body in shape and decide to exercise each day before work. Your alarm goes off the first day and you are half-awake. It feels so good—so right—to stay in bed. What do you do? You cross your will and decide, "I am going to get out of bed, get dressed and head to the gym." You have to cross your will even though the bed feels so good and so right. Later that night at a restaurant as you look over the menu, there are several entrees that look so good, but are high in fat and calories. However, because of your physical discipline, you say, "No! I am going to have to cross my will and eat something healthier." Finally, you decide to hire a personal trainer, who will have some degree of authority over you and your training. You work under his supervision, and he may tell you to do one more set on the bench press.

Do you see what is happening? There are many experiences in this life that feel good and right but, over time, they can harm your health. Therefore you are willing to have your will crossed. Physical health and physical freedom come by finding the right restrictions.

This is the paradoxical nature of true, positive freedom. It is knowing the right restrictions, setting boundaries, saying "no" to yourself so you can build a good physique, strength and stamina. You are forfeiting something of value for the sake of something of greater value. This is what Berlin meant by positive freedom.

Positive freedom is also at work in the moral and spiritual realm. We were made to operate a certain way. God designed life so that it is governed by certain laws and principles, and if we live in harmony with them, our lives will flourish. For this reason, a life full of foolish and unwise choices is not freedom. As Guinness rightly observes:

> Freedom is not choice so much as right choice, good choice and wise choice. When everything is permissible, no one is truly free, so it is ironic but not accidental that millions in 'the land of the free' are in recovery groups from one addiction or another.

Author Ronald Macaulay gives some great insight into the relationship between law and freedom:

> [God's law] helps us to see how we are made to function. For obviously, if we are made to live in a certain way, and we live against that design, we make life difficult for ourselves. It is a little like treating plants, or animals or even machines according to their design. We have to find out the proper environment, temperature, food, attitudes, fuel, etcetera, that each requires— then, as we respect these design factors, things work, plants are healthy and produce flowers and fruit, animals are healthy and obedient, machines run smoothly.
>
> The same is true for humans. We are designed in a certain way, both physically and spiritually. Therefore, the closer we get to living consistently with His design, the better and freer we are. This is how the law has a positive function. This is why we must respect it, search for it and receive it gladly, even when it contradicts previously held opinions.

This is the way God intended it to be, and this is what leads to our ultimate well-being.

3.2

Freedom Without Restrictions

I ATTENDED COLLEGE at the University of the South in Sewanee, Tennessee. It sits on top of a mountain in Middle Tennessee, surrounded by magnificent, breathtaking views and serene calmness.

When I was a student, there was a local physician who owned a glider and would get my roommate, Fred, to help him launch his plane. They would go to the small, local airport and Fred would pull the plane down the runway via an old station wagon. They had to reach a speed of up to 90 miles per hour before the doctor could release the cable and the plane take flight. It was almost the perfect picture of freedom, as it silently soared over the mountain. At times, on a sunny day, I would walk on campus and see a shadow soundlessly flash over me. It was the glider plane, a picture of beauty that flew effortlessly and free.

But, why is the glider plane able to soar? It seems to have no restrictions. Yet, in reality, it is not because of a lack of restrictions, it is because the plane is honoring the aerodynamic realities of air currents. The glider was built for air currents, which is the environment in which it soars. If you put it in the water, it would sink. Freedom is not a lack of restriction, it is finding the right restrictions that fit your being and lead to harmony, peace and joy in your life.

One of the best ways to understand freedom and restrictions is to consider the game of football, a sport that provides incredible entertainment value, whether you play or watch as a spectator. The game is governed by rules, and for the sake of this illustration, we are going to call the rules the "Law of the Game." It is the "Law of the Game" that makes the game and gives it order. The game makes no sense without the "Law of the Game."

One day, suppose those on the committee who make the rules are pressured by modern thinkers to make some changes. They are told the rules are too restrictive and the players need more freedom to do what they do best. They truly believe it would make the game more exciting and enjoyable for both the players and the fans, so they enact three changes to the "Law of the Game." First, since it is so difficult to determine whether a face mask penalty is intentional or unintentional, they do away with the penalty. Face masks can now be grabbed. Second, since so many holding calls are hard to detect and are often missed by referees, they decide to do away with holding penalties. Anyone can now hold anyplace at any time. Finally, to add more excitement to the return game, they enact a rule that allows one to block in the back on kickoff and punt returns. They make these changes to the "Law of the Game" in the name of freedom. It would bring more enjoyment and pleasure to the game.

Now, if you know and understand the game of football, you know that removing these restrictions would lead to an incredible number of injuries. But, more significantly, the game would devolve into chaos. This is what happens when you have freedom with no restrictions. This explains why lives are so chaotic in a culture that is so free. And it explains all the unhappiness in our land.

If you go back to the parable and think about the game of football, what makes the game so enjoyable is that you have certain restrictions. You must instill the law of the game and you have to have obedience to the law. Within the "Law of the Game," there is great freedom. You can run whatever scheme you desire. On offense you can be conservative or run a hurry-up, no-huddle offense. You can go for it on fourth down or choose otherwise. You can run trick plays. Defensively, you can run any type of defense. You can blitz, you can run a three-four or a four-three. Ultimately, you can be as free and creative as your heart desires, but only within the "Law of the Game." This is what gives the game order and provides such enjoyment to the players and fans.

This is how God designed life to work. Freedom with no restrictions will cause us to crash and burn. Freedom within God's law, the law that was given to us by the One who designed us, will lead to peace, order and harmony. It is a key to finding happiness.

3.3

Freedom and the Pursuit of Happiness

FURTHER RESEARCHING the concept of freedom and what it means to be free, it struck me that there are two ways to approach life: to submit my life to God and His will, or to seek to be free to do whatever I want to do. Said another way, it's *Thy will be done vs. my will be done.* The second approach clearly has undeniable appeal. After all, it is only natural to want to do your own thing.

I have concluded that many Americans believe freedom means the absence of restraints in our lives. As long as we can follow our hearts and as long as we do not hurt anyone, this is the key to a full and happy life—to fulfill all of our yearnings and desires.

If you look around the world today, this modern view of freedom is clearly not working. It does not lead to happiness, and it never will, because this way of thinking inevitably breaks down. It leads to chaos and pain. In fact, I would say this model of freedom explains why people's lives are not working in a progressive culture that seems to have it all.

One of the main reasons today's view of freedom breaks down is because of our failure to understand the complexity of the human heart and its design.

We believe we are only free if we can do whatever our heart wants. But, have you ever noticed the competing desires in your life and how they can be so contradictory? For example, if you want to be healthy, fit and live a long life, but you also smoke cigarettes and drink heavily, at some point you realize your model breaks down. The competing interests require that you choose a side, and you finally understand freedom is not the ability to do whatever you want, as your desires can be endless, easily colliding with each another.

Author Philip Yancey shares an interesting story about his older brother, an incredibly gifted musician.

> In an attempt to break the shackles of a confining upbringing, he went on a grand quest for freedom, trying on worldviews like changes of clothing: Pentecostalism, atheistic existentialism, Buddhism, New Age Spirituality, Thomistic rationalism. He joined the flower children of the 1960s, growing his hair long and wearing granny glasses, living communally, experimenting with sex and drugs. For a time he sent me exuberant reports of his new life. Eventually, however, a darker side crept in. I had to bail him out of jail when an LSD trip went bad. He broke relations with every other person in the family, and he burned through several marriages. I got late-night suicide calls. Watching my brother, I learned that apparent freedom can actually mask deep bondage, a cry from the heart of unmet needs. The most musically gifted person I have ever known ended up tuning pianos, not playing them on a concert stage.

Yancey had a front row seat to witness the destructive power of a life in unrestrained freedom. Had his brother genuinely wanted to become an accomplished musician and play in concert halls, it would have required hours and hours of practice. This would have restricted the freedom he craved, although the discipline and hard work would have unleashed his immeasurable talent to produce beautiful music that otherwise lay dormant.

In the book of James (1:25), we find insightful words on freedom. He speaks of the person "who looks intently into the perfect law that gives freedom." Yet, how could that be true, that God's perfect law leads to our freedom? It would seem to be the opposite—that God's law would take our freedom away from us. There are many who see God as one who desires to steal our happiness.

I would ask you to consider what James has written from a different perspective. New York City pastor Tim Keller says that sometimes you have to deliberately give up your freedom to engage in activities and thought processes that will enable you to release yourself to a richer kind of freedom. And as we look at the competing desires of our hearts, it is critical for us to discover which of our desires are liberating and which are destructive. Ultimately, we need to determine which of our desires are aligned with who we really are, and therefore, enhance our lives.

In our quest for happiness, it is crucial we recognize that freedom is not a lack of restrictions; rather, it is finding the *right* restrictions. Freedom occurs when you discover the restrictions that best fit your being and lead to harmony, peace and joy in your life.

3.4

Freedom and the Pursuit of Happiness, Part 2

W E HAVE EXPLORED how much of today's society believes happiness is found by being free from restrictions. As long as we can follow our hearts wherever they lead, and as long as we do not hurt anyone, our culture says this is the key to a full and happy life.

Contradicting this notion, however, is the complexity of the human heart, which causes this modern view of freedom to break down and ultimately fails us.

Another reason this model collapses is due to the complexity of motivation. Many never stop and ask, "Why do I do what I do? What is it that drives my life? What is most important to me?"

One of my favorite books is Stephen Covey's *The Seven Habits of Highly Effective People*. Covey says that each of us has a "personal center." He adds, "Whatever is at the center of our life will be the source of our security, guidance, wisdom and power."

Covey continues to make his point that every aspect of someone's life is determined by his or her personal center. One way to understand this is to realize everyone lives for something. There is one thing that gives us a sense of significance and security. It is what makes us feel valuable and grounded, knowing that our lives are worth something. We believe that without this one thing, there is no way to be happy.

Covey says specifically that we can be money-centered, work-centered, pleasure-centered, success-centered, family-centered or God-centered. There is one main thing in our lives that makes us feel worthwhile and full of meaning. But, what we don't realize is that whatever is at our personal center becomes our master. You have given yourself to it, you are under its control and, therefore, you are not free. As an example, some individuals are workaholics, as money, status or achievement is at their personal center, which controls them. Others enter bad relationships and stay in them even though, on an intellectual level, they know that they should not continue. They have a great need for romance and the presence of a significant person in their lives.

No one is free. You might think you are in control and are your own person, but you are not. As the Greek philosopher, Euripedes, who lived 2,500 years ago said, "No one is truly free." You can serve either wealth or the law, or you can serve the people you are seeking to please. We do not control ourselves; we are controlled by that which is at the center of our being.

In the New Testament, the Apostle Paul brings this into the spiritual realm. He states there are two types of people in the world–those who unconditionally serve God with their lives, and those who spiritually are slaves to something else. There are no other choices.

Bob Buford, a prosperous businessman and founder of Halftime Ministries, shares the conversation that changed his life:

A turning point in my own life was a conversation that I had 20 years ago with Michael Kami, one of this country's top strategic planners. . . I made an appointment with Mike to explore my own (future) plans. I wanted to get his personal advice about some of the options that I was examining. During the course of the conversation, Mike asked me to describe my basic interests and motivations, and so I began telling him about the things that interested me. But, suddenly Mike stopped me in midsentence and asked me a question that changed my life.

"What's in the box?"

The question took me by surprise. I didn't get it at first. In the box? What does that mean? So I asked, "What do you mean by that, Mike?"

"What's central to your life at this point?" Mike asked. "If there were room for only one thing in your life, what would it be?" He took a pencil and sketched out a small square on a sheet of paper and said, "From what you're telling me, Bob, there are two things at the top of your list of priorities, your religious faith and your career." Mike indicated that the shorthand for that was a dollar sign and a cross. And he pointed at the box and said, "Before I can help you focus your interests, you have to decide: What's in the box?"

Would it be the dollar sign or the cross? Suddenly I knew I had a choice to make.

Now and then, in the midst of life's complexities, we come to a point where the options are limited and clear. This was one of those moments. What would it be for me—more money, more success or more energy transferred to the calling I sensed so strongly? I considered those two options for a minute or so— which seemed like an eternity—and then I said, "Well, if you put it that way, it's the cross." And then I reached over to pencil a cross into Mike's box.

That one decision helped me frame everything I've done since that day. It wasn't that the small cross indicated that the work I felt called to do, to serve God, was my only loyalty in life. There were also family, customers, employees, recreation and the like, but that little cross has designated the primary loyalty for my life between then and now.

My final thought is that Jesus is a king. In fact, He is the King of all kings. Clearly, if we don't choose Him to be our King, we will choose another king. It is not a matter of freedom, it is a matter of who or what will be the Lord of our lives. We will submit to some*one* or to some*thing*.

The great irony is this—Jesus is the only legitimate king. He is the only king that truly liberates those who choose to serve Him.

4

WISDOM IN THE SEARCH FOR MEANING

Meaning is not a luxury for us, it is a kind of spiritual oxygen that enables our souls to live.

--Dr. Dallas Willard

4.1

The Search for
Meaning in Life

THE EARLY GREEK philosophers taught that all human beings are "telic" creatures. Telic comes from the Greek word, *telos*, which means *purpose*. They believed we are all purpose-driven, meaning-seeking creatures.

I consider them to be right. We all have to live for something. We all believe deep in our hearts, whether we are aware of it or not, there is something in the world that makes us complete and whole, giving our lives meaning.

Writer Emily Esfahani Smith published a superb magazine article in *The Atlantic*, explaining why meaning in life is more important than happiness.

She focused her research on Victor Frankl and his classic best-selling book, *Man's Search for Meaning*. Many consider it to be one of the most influential books ever published in the United States.

Frankl was a prominent Jewish psychiatrist and neurologist who lived in Vienna, Austria. In 1942, he and his wife and parents were arrested and transported to a Nazi concentration camp. At the end of the war three years later, Frankl was set free, though his wife and parents did not survive. Following four years of recovery and reflection, Frankl spent nine days writing *Man's Search for Meaning*. In sharing his experiences in a Nazi death camp, Frankl concluded that the difference between those who had lived and those who had died came down to one thing—meaning.

Frankl recognized that seeking to find a meaningful life is at odds with a culture that is much more interested in the pursuit of happiness.

"It is a characteristic of the American culture that, again and again," said Frankl, "one is commanded and ordered to be happy." Frankl concludes that happiness is a by-product of leading a meaningful life. That is why Frankl believed the actual pursuit of happiness is what thwarts our ability to find it.

Furthermore, research clearly demonstrates that living with a sense of purpose and meaning increases a person's overall well-being, which includes life satisfaction, mental health and self-esteem. Most significantly, a meaningful life decreases the chances of suffering from depression.

It is troubling that modern civilization has a hard time finding meaning in life. People are empty, only attaining brief moments of pleasure in life, but finding no meaning.

In the four essays to follow, I hope to reveal positive insight into where we can find meaning in this one life we are given.

4.2

Why Are We Here?

A S WE CONSIDER the meaning in life, the best place to start is with the subject of worldview, or the lens through which we view life.

Dr. Armand Nicholi, a psychiatrist who teaches at Harvard Medical School, writes that your worldview determines your view of purpose in life.

> It helps us understand where we come from, our heritage; who we are, our identity, why we exist on this planet, our purpose.

Several years ago, *Life* publications came out with a book on how individuals coped in their quests to find meaning in life. The writers and researchers interviewed a cross-section of society, from architects and philosophers to plumbers and those dealing with substance addictions.

Here are the words of a New York City taxi driver as he explains his godless view of the meaning of life:

> We're here to die, just live and die. I live driving a cab. I do some fishing, take my girl out, pay taxes, do a little reading, then get ready to drop dead. Life is a big fake. . . . You're rich or you're poor. You're here, you're gone. You're like the wind. After you're gone, other people will come. It's too late to make it better. Everyone's fed up, can't believe in nothing no more. People have

no pride. People have no fear. People only care about one thing and that's money. We're gonna destroy ourselves, nothing we can do about it. The only cure for the world's illness is nuclear war—wipe everything out and start over. We've become like a cornered animal, fighting for survival. Life is nothing.

Let me now contrast this taxi driver with another driver I met while in New York City several years ago.

I was rushing to a meeting when I hailed a cab and hurriedly gave the address to the driver. The unassuming man was probably in his sixties and appeared to be short of stature. He wore thick eyeglasses and spoke with a decidedly foreign accent. I could see that he was kind and friendly, although he initially spoke few words to me.

I settled into the back seat when I noticed a yellow bumper sticker staring me in the face. It was attached to the back side of the front seat's head-rest. The sticker simply read, "Jews for Jesus." I knew this to be a national organization of Jewish people who had converted to Christianity. However, I acted somewhat naïve and asked him to tell me about the meaning of the words on his not-so-subtle bumper sticker. Surprisingly, that was like flipping a switch from 'off' to 'on' as he joyfully told me his story.

He had been a practicing Jew until he realized the prophecies in the Old Testament, those that pointed to the Jewish Messiah, were clearly pointing to the man whom Christians call Jesus.

As we drove down Fifth Avenue, it dawned on me that he was evangelizing me. I finally shared that I was a Christian, and we were on the same team.

We finally arrived at my destination, and as I was getting out my wallet to pay the fare, he said something to me I will never forget:

God has blessed me. He has called me to drive a cab in New York City. Every day I get to serve people and drive them around the city, and every day I have the opportunity to share the good news of the gospel. I am a blessed man.

Here you have two men in similar roles: both provide the same, essential and valued service in a vibrant city that is arguably the economic capital of the world's most prosperous nation. Yet, despite the similarities, they are obviously different in how they go about their jobs. Both have radically different worldviews and divergent perspectives on life. As such, they are planting different seeds and harvesting different fruits.

Secularism does not have much to offer human beings when it comes to purpose in life. Actor and film director Woody Allen, an avowed atheist, continually laments the terrible emptiness of life:

> . . . alienation, loneliness and emptiness verging on madness. The fundamental things behind all motivation and all activity is the constant struggle against annihilation and against death. It's absolutely stupefying in its terror, and it renders anyone's accomplishments meaningless.

Finding meaning and purpose is a question that reaches all the way back to the Greek philosophers. They believed in a concept called the *logos*. It is where we get the English word *logic*. In Greek, the word *logos* literally means "the word," but it has a secondary meaning, "the reason for life." The Greeks believed that when one found his *logos*— his reason for life—he would be complete and whole, able to reach his full potential as a person.

The problem is that the Greeks could never agree on what comprised the *logos*. They could never construct a unified belief on the reason for life. Rather than being "the word," *logos* became nothing more than "just another word."

Tim Keller says this is why the apostle John, in his opening words in the gospel of John, drops a bombshell on the world:

> *In the beginning was the Logos, and the Logos was with God, and the Logos was God. He was with God in the beginning. All things came into being through Him, and apart from Him nothing came into being that has come into being. Life was in Him, and that life was the light of men. That light shines in the darkness, Yet the darkness did not overcome it (John 1:1-5, author paraphrase).*

God is revealing to us that in the beginning was the *logos*, the reason for life; and the reason for life was God, and the reason became a human being and dwelt among us. What John says is that the *logos,* the reason for life, was not and is not a philosophical principle as the Greeks believed; rather, the *logos* is, in fact, the person Jesus Christ.

When we enter into a relationship with Him and truly get to know Him and serve Him, we become complete and whole. We find a higher purpose for which to live. It is in Jesus Christ, indeed, that we discover our reason for life.

4.3

Finding Meaning in a Chaotic World

WHEN PRESIDENT Bill Clinton occupied the White House, he participated in a press conference aired on MTV. It was intended to be light and funny as he interacted with teens. You may recall, Clinton was asked humorous, trivial questions such as, "What is your favorite rock group? What kind of underwear; boxers or briefs?"

But, out of the blue, 17-year-old Dahlia Schweitzer dared to ask a more thought-provoking question:

> Mr. President, it seems to me that Kurt Cobain's (lead singer of the rock group Nirvana) recent suicide exemplified the emptiness that many in our generation feel. What would you say to our generation about this?

President Clinton was visibly floored and did not know how to respond. He finally found an answer he thought suitable and basically told the young girl that everyone is important to each other in this life.

So, there Schweitzer stood, asking the president of the United States to comment on the emptiness and meaninglessness of life that her generation faced, and one of the most influential men in the world did not have an answer.

I believe there is something terribly wrong in our culture, because people do not understand the reason for their earthly existence.

One of my favorite authors is Dr. Peter Kreeft. He is 79 years of age and still teaches philosophy at Boston College. He has written 48 books, with one of them stating:

> "We are the first civilization that does not know why we exist. Every past civilization has had some religious answer to that question. The essence of modernity is the abandonment of that religious foundation."

In essence, Kreeft is explaining why modern people find life to be empty and meaningless. If there is no God that stands behind our earthly existence, life is pointless.

All great atheist thinkers will tell you that, since there is no God and no designer who brought life into being,

1. There is no grand purpose.
2. Life is ultimately meaningless.
3. We are all alone in this vast universe.
4. When we die, we go into everlasting nothingness.

If you are honest, you have to admit this is a bleak way of looking at life.

British novelist C. S. Lewis expressed that the pessimism and gloom he experienced the first 31 years of his life was clearly related to his atheistic worldview. His life as a Christian was full of joy and vibrancy because his life had meaning and purpose.

A week before he died, Lewis declared, "I have done all that I was sent in the world to do, and I am ready to go."

What a stark contrast to Woody Allen, who many consider to be the greatest movie director of all time.

In a recent interview with *The New York Times*, Allen said, "I still lie awake at night terrified of the void." He is speaking of the difficulty he has reconciling his strident atheism with all that he observes in the real world.

Allen admits, "I make movies not to make any type of grand statement, but simply to take my mind off the existential horror of being alive."

As depressing as this sounds, it is the natural outworking of a godless view of life.

You may be thinking this does not apply to you because you believe in God. However, in this secular age that we live in, a majority of people believe in God and the spiritual world, but He is irrelevant to our day-to-day living, and He does not impact our view of life and our search for meaning.

It has been said that "we are predominately a nation of practical atheists, in that, we believe in God, but live as if He does not exist."

A good question we should all stop and consider: "Does God play a role in helping me find purpose and meaning in life?" What I have learned is that many of us are like Woody Allen, who finds diversion in movie making to keep himself from having to think about all of this.

I consider this to be true for many of us as well. We seek to divert our minds with work and the pleasures of life, to keep us from having to think about the emptiness of life, and that one day this is all going to end.

When we connect with God vertically, we find meaning horizontally in the world in which we live. As the Apostle Paul states: "In Christ we are made complete."

4.4

Harvard: Our Culture in Microcosm

A S WE CONTINUE to peel away the complexities and questions that encompass our journey for wisdom, this chapter is highly important and revealing as it relates to our ability to find meaning in life.

First of all, it is essential to define the word "microcosm." The simplest definition is "something that is seen as a small version of something much larger." Through this one concept, I hope to illustrate how Harvard University, the great educational institution, is a small version of what is happening in Western culture.

In addition, I must declare that I have no ax to grind with Harvard. I stumbled upon this idea from two books I read. The first book was *The Question of God* by Dr. Armand Nicholi, a professor of psychiatry at Harvard Medical School, who also taught a popular undergraduate level course at Harvard for 35 years. The second book was *Finding God Beyond Harvard* by Kelly Kullberg, founder of the Veritas Forum at Harvard, where she served as a chaplain to students.

Harvard was founded in 1636 and one of its central bylaws was:

"Let every student be earnestly pressed to consider well that the main end of his life and studies is to know God and Jesus Christ who is eternal life–and therefore to lay Christ in the bottom, as the only foundation of all sound knowledge and learning."

There is no doubt that Harvard was a spiritually vibrant place for years. In fact, various groups and individuals believe this was the foundation that lead to its initial greatness as an educational institution.

That has all changed. It appears today that Jesus has been expelled from the institution. When Henri Nouwen resigned from Harvard Divinity School in 1985, he described the place as a spiritual desert, that God was dead at Harvard, even at the divinity school.

In February of 1993, American Christian evangelist Billy Graham conducted a lengthy meeting with Harvard's president, Derek Bok. As Graham was leaving, he asked Bok one last question, "What is the number one struggle the students at Harvard have to contend with?" Bok had no need to give it much thought, as he quickly responded, "Living with emptiness."

Upon hearing this, Kullberg asked the question, "How did such a great institution like Harvard become a place of emptiness?"

Dr. Nicholi often asked his class of undergraduates if they and the people around them were happy. Invariably, they answered "no." When he asked them why they found their lives to be so unhappy, they generally responded it was because of a lack of meaning in their lives and relationships.

Kullberg shares a shocking incident upon attempting to reach out and minister to a few of the women at Harvard Divinity School. She attended a women's meeting that was held in the University Chapel, called the Full Moon Circle. The group described themselves as a Neopagan, pre-Christian, ecofeminist Wiccan society. Of course, Wiccan Societies practice witchcraft.

Kullberg describes the chapel as packed and the women chanted to the spirits, worshipped the full moon and many attempted to reach their dead ancestors. It was shocking to see these bright, educated women acting as if they were unenlightened pagans.

In 2006, the cover story of Harvard's student newspaper, *The Crimson,* revealed the rampant incidence of student depression amongst the university's 6,700 students. The newspaper reported that 80 percent of the student body had experienced depression at least once during the school year. Nearly half (47 percent) of the student body found themselves depressed to the point of having a hard time functioning. Ten percent (650 students) had strongly considered committing suicide.

Nobel Prize winning French novelist Albert Camus said, "There is but one truly philosophical problem, and that is suicide. Judging whether life is worth living amounts to answering the fundamental question of philosophy." Camus knew of many people who took their lives because they saw life to be meaningless and, therefore not worth living.

Thomas Masaryk, the first president of liberated Czechoslovakia after World War I, wrote the book, *Suicide and the Meaning of Civilization*. The thesis of the book states that the more godless a society becomes, the higher the rate of suicide. His research suggests that in the Middle Ages, the number of suicides was negligible. By the end of the nineteenth century, suicide had become one of the top causes of death. Today, suicide has surpassed car crashes as the leading cause of death due to injury. Furthermore, Masaryk uncovered that the vast majority of these deaths occurred among highly principled, well-educated people who had no religious faith. His conclusion reveals the tragic story of those individuals who can find no purpose in life and, therefore have no reason to live.

To acquire meaning, you have to look to God to answer the significant questions of life. These questions concern our place and purpose in the world, the significance of our lives, and our ultimate destiny. Unfortunately, much of our population has moved away from the Biblical worldview that has always supplied the answers to these questions. But, the questions have not gone away and they never will. Modern man is therefore left all alone, disconnected from the One who gives life meaning.

4.5

Answering Life's
Big Questions

JOHN O'NEIL has served as president of the Californian School of Professional Psychology and consults with chief executive officers of major corporations. He wrote the fascinating book, *The Paradox of Success*. O'Neil is clearly not a man of faith, but shares insightful words about finding meaning in life:

> The basic questions we encounter when we look deeply into the shadow are spiritual questions. They concern our place and purpose in the world, the significance of our lives, and our personal connection to whatever force keeps the world humming along. Most of us today have moved away from the religious structures that once supplied answers to these questions, but the questions have not gone away. Our compulsive busyness, our dread of unstructured time, and our reluctance to be alone with ourselves are rooted in the uncomfortable sense that our lives lack meaning, that we are disconnected and alone.

O'Neil is referring to the big questions of life, which he admits are spiritual, and they never go away. They are always confronting us. He imparts we have "moved away from the religious structures that once supplied answers to these questions. And where does that leave us?" Disconnected and alone, with a life that lacks meaning.

So, what are the big questions that human beings have always asked? Though there are many, I am going to limit them to three.

Who am I?
Why am I here?
What is my ultimate destiny when this life is over?

When you "move away from the religious structures" to answer these questions (as O'Neil put it), you end up with no real answers. If there is no God, we are here by chance. We are nothing but a mass of molecules. A human life has no real value for we are nothing but a product of nature. Since we are just physical beings, we have no souls or any spiritual dimension to our lives. We are meaningless beings in this random universe.

Why are we here? There is no reason for our earthly existence, because we are here by chance. Therefore our lives are pointless, because there is no God who endowed our lives with a purpose.

Finally, when you die, your body decays, and you go into everlasting nothingness. You cease to exist.

It is somewhat apparent that, as we become more secular and godless, our outlook on the future becomes more gloomy and bleak, because there is no meaning in life. This explains why the depression rate is 10 times higher today than it was 50 years ago, and why suicide has surpassed car crashes as the leading cause of death due to injury.

When we go back to the three big questions, you learn that the Christian response is clearly different. It provides answers that give our earthly lives a sense of meaning and coherence.

Who are we? We are creatures designed in the image of God, which means we possess a number of God's characteristics. We possess an immortal soul, which makes us unique and of infinite value compared to animal life.

Our value as people is not based on what we do, what we achieve, or how successful we are. It is based clearly on the One who made us and put us here.

Why are we here? In other words, what is the reason God put us here? What is the reason for my earthly existence?

When you look at our design, it is clear we have been given the ability to love. We are naturally relational beings. We are told:

. . . all things have been created by Him and for Him. (Colossians 1:16)

. . . we exist for Him . . ." (I Corinthians 8:6)

God put us here to connect with Him, to have a relationship with Him, to know Him and to love Him.

When you think about it, it is similar to why we have children. We bring children into the world, anticipating a loving, life-long relationship with them. This is what God anticipates with us.

Finally, *what is my ultimate destiny once this life ends? Is there life after this life?*

The main theme of the Bible is the answer to this question. If you read the four gospels in the New Testament, you will notice two phrases that Jesus uses over and over. These phrases are:

Eternal Life
The Kingdom of God

Notice that Jesus places special emphasis on the importance of obtaining eternal life and entering the Kingdom of God.

He makes it obvious that you enter through Him. He is the door. He is the way. As we put our faith in Him, we are allowed to enter.

So, what is our final destiny? *Eternal life in the kingdom of God through Jesus Christ.*

These are the answers to life's big questions. Christianity answers them all. This is why the Christian faith gives such coherence to this life, as it provides the path to a meaningful life, and hope as we look to the future and, ultimately the end of our earthly life.

BUSINESS AND CAREER
WISDOM

*Whenever an individual's talents have been discovered,
developed and used for the good of others, some measure of
true success has been achieved.*
—Dr. Thomas Morris

5.1

Business Wisdom

L AST YEAR I met with a bright business consultant from out of town, whom I connected with through a mutual friend. During our visit, the consultant asked me if I knew of any companies in our community that might be interested in using his services. Before responding, I asked him what set him and his firm apart from other consulting firms competing in the marketplace. I was greatly impressed with his answer.

He told me that, to be a successful business, there are two essential components. First, you have to be smart. In other words, you want to have a good business strategy, state-of-the-art technology and effective marketing. This includes being well-capitalized and having a strong sales function.

Secondly, you have to be a healthy company. You want high morale, a real sense of unity, good communication, minimum politics and a low turnover rate among employees.

He then explained that most companies and consulting firms focus on being smart, but his firm spends its time helping companies become healthy.

From my experience in the business world and from counseling businessmen, these words ring true. It is natural to create a smart, well-run business and in the process fail to pay sufficient attention to the health of your company and the relationships that exist among the employees.

American Christian author Philip Yancey tells the story of one of his good friends who worked as a consultant in the corporate world. At a certain point, he evaluated the courses he had taken and taught on the principles of good leadership and management. It occurred to him he had never taken a course on how to love, even though the Bible presents it as the primary command in life. So, he gathered a group of people together and asked them to think about one question: "When have I felt loved?" The responses were telling:

When someone listens attentively to me, when someone makes me feel important, when someone encourages me, when someone respectfully challenges me, when someone cares for me when I am hurting, or when somebody gives me an unexpected gift.

Yancey's friend then took a few of his clients through this same exercise, including one female executive who worked within a dysfunctional company. Although her company discouraged fraternizing, she began going down the hall, stopping in offices to visit her employees. She had no real agenda for any visit. The first person was terrified, thinking she had come into his office to fire him. "No, no," she said, "I just figured that after three years of working together, I should get to know you."

She spent time with all 13 of her employees until her boss called her in one day.

"I don't know what the hell you're doing," he said, "but this company was almost bankrupt. It has turned around, and when I asked our people what had happened, everybody said that you were responsible."

This reminds me of what someone once told me long ago:

Your employees will be totally committed to you and the mission of the company if they know you truly care for them.

I don't know about you, but my instincts tell me that to be an exceptional organization, you clearly have to be smart, but maybe even more importantly, you have to be healthy.

5.2

Career and Achievement

I HAVE OFTEN wondered why the suicide rate for men is so much higher than it is for women. Eight out of 10 suicides are by men, a significant difference. Knowing this, I have concluded that women must be much healthier than men. In my view, they have much better friendships and relationships and they are transparent with each other.

Julie Scelfo, a talented journalist with *The New York Times*, wrote an interesting article on men and depression that became the lead article in *Newsweek*. She commented that millions of men each year are diagnosed with depression, but that millions more suffer silently, reluctant to own up to their condition. Instead of openly talking about their pain, they mask it with alcohol, prescription or illegal drugs, gambling, anger, or the all-American attribute of workaholism. Scelfo wastes no time getting to the heart of the matter:

> . . . *when they do realize that they have a problem, men often view asking for help as an admission of weakness, a betrayal of their male identities.*

So, why is there such a proliferation of suicide among men? I think we can reasonably conclude that men now suffer much greater from depression than they have in the past. But, why?

I am sure there are plenty of factors involved to determine risks for depression. Based on the work I do with men, I see one overriding issue that creates all types of internal struggles which, ultimately, lead to depression.

Our culture is one where a man obtains his sense of worth based on how well he performs in his occupation. Dr. Tim Keller suggests that ours is the first culture in history where men define themselves solely by performing and achieving in the workplace. It is the way a man becomes *somebody*. Dr. Keller adds that he believes there has never been greater psychological, social and emotional pressure in the marketplace than there is at this exact moment.

For many men today, life is about "what I do," and "how successful I am at what I do." Over time this causes us to wonder, "What do you think about what I do? How do you rate what I do?" Through this way of thinking, it is only a matter of time before I begin to worry, "What if I fail at what I do? What would the people in my sphere of influence think of me?"

Fear of failure is one of man's greatest fears. It is like a psychological death. In his first interview from prison, former investment advisor and fraudster Bernie Madoff said he was motivated to pull off this grand Ponzi scheme because he feared failure. As he put it, "I did not want to lose the honor and esteem of men."

David Sokol was considered by many to be the person who would one day replace Warren Buffett as the CEO of Berkshire Hathaway. That was before he was forced to resign because of unethical conduct. Sokol was driven to rise up the corporate ladder because of his unbelievable work ethic, largely because of fear of failing.

In another instance, an extremely wealthy businessman confided in me that every day his feet hit the floor, he is motivated by one thing: fear of failure. It seems that most men are not driven to succeed, they are driven *not to fail*. They are not running toward something; rather they are sprinting *away* from failure.

One of the main reasons men fear failure with such great intensity is because of the shame it generates. Shame, according to popular lecturer Malcolm Smith, is "the leukemia of masculinity." Shame causes men to hide their fears and faults. If we believe we do not have what it takes to be a man, that we are inadequate and do not measure up, it invalidates our sense of manhood.

Shame is what destroys men's lives, and failure is at its root.

Fortunately, there is a way to come to terms with this. Charles Cooley, a prominent and highly respected sociologist who lived from 1864 to 1929, developed a landmark concept known as *the looking glass self*, a human development theory which remains valid today. In its simplest form, the theory states:

> A person gets his identity in life based on how the most important person in his life sees him.

For an adult man, particularly out in the workplace, the opinion valued most generally comes from colleagues and people within the community he lives. We allow them to make the final verdict on the value of our lives. It explains why we always wonder, "What do people think of me?"

What do you think would happen to a man if Jesus Christ became the most important person in his life?

If He were the audience whom we sought to please the most, it would truly change everything, for we are of great value to Him, and He loves us with an everlasting love. His love does not depend on how well we perform or our level of achievement.

This is what happened to C. S. Lewis when he converted from atheism to Christianity. In Christ, he found a new identity. He described it as "coming to terms with his real personality."

Furthermore, Lewis added, "Until you have given yourself up to Him, you will never find your true self."

Only when Jesus Christ becomes the firm foundation in our lives will we discover who we are and what our lives are all about.

5.3

Why Leaders Fail

AUTHOR STEPHEN COVEY often spoke of how leadership development has changed. He shared that all relevant literature on leadership written from 1776 to 1925 emphasized the importance of character. It focused on "The Character Ethic" as the foundation of success, with emphasis on character traits such as humility, integrity, fidelity and courage. Covey said that the character ethic "taught that there are basic principles of effective living, and that people can only experience true success and enduring happiness as they learn and integrate these principles into their basic character."

He later noticed a shift in the literature about leadership and success, stating, "I began to feel more and more that much of the success literature of the past 50 years was superficial. It was filled with social image consciousness, techniques and quick fixes."

I would imagine we are witnessing how the loss of this "character ethic," as Covey called it, is playing out in the lives of the business and political leaders today.

Several years ago, an article appeared in the *Harvard Business Review* on why leaders in various business organizations fail. The core data came from a study revealing the four primary factors attributing to the failures of those senior leaders:

- They were *authoritarian*—controlling, demanding and not listening to others.

- They were *autonomous*—aloof, isolated and reflecting little accountability.
- They committed *adultery*.
- They became more and more *arrogant*.

The underlying reason these leaders encountered failure could be summed up by these words from the study: "feeling and acting as if they were superior to all others." If you think you are superior to everyone in your organization, you will find yourself thinking you can treat people however you want, sleep with whomever you choose, and spend the organization's money at will. Basically, you believe you can do whatever you want.

This is what arrogance does to a person's life and what makes people weak, ineffective leaders. Making it even more devastating is that arrogant people are not aware of their arrogance. Others clearly see it and are repelled by it, but the arrogant person is totally blind to it himself.

A number of years ago, Jim Collins, a faculty member at the Stanford University Graduate School of Business, wrote a best-selling book, *Built to Last*. It was based on a management study of companies he and his associates performed in the 1990s with the intent of analyzing and demonstrating how great companies sustain themselves over time.

In studying the data, Collins created the idea of determining if certain universal characteristics distinguished truly great companies. Using tough benchmarks, Collins and his research team identified 11 elite companies (including Abbott Labs, Kimberly Clark and Nucor Steel) doing a good job and had somehow produced phenomenal results for 15 consecutive years. He and his team sought to establish how these companies made the leap from being *good* companies to being *great* companies. Collins took the collective results of his intensive research and wrote *Good to Great*, which became one of the best-selling business books ever published.

What I find interesting is that Collins gave his research team explicit instructions to downplay the role of top executives, as he did not believe the business community needed another book on leadership. Yet, although he had insisted they ignore the role of the company executives, the research team kept pushing back. After going back and forth, as Collins put it, "the data won."

They recognized that all the executives from these good-to-great companies were cut from the same cloth. They were each what he called a "Level 5 Leader."

Collins concluded, "Level 5 Leaders are a study in duality: modest and willful, humble and fearless." These good-to-great leaders never desired to be celebrities or to be lifted up on a pedestal. Collins declared they were "seemingly ordinary people quietly producing extraordinary results." What Collins and his team of researchers clearly observed is that a Level 5 Leader builds enduring greatness through the paradoxical blend of personal humility and professional will.

I profoundly believe the greatest character trait a leader can possess is humility.

5.4

Strength is Found in Humility

OUR LAST ESSAY ended with a quote from Jim Collin's best-selling book, *Good to Great.* Collins and his team of researchers observed that "Level 5 Leaders build enduring greatness through the paradoxical blend of personal humility and professional will."

Christian apologist Tim Keller makes a similar observation when he declares:

> *The humble are kind and gentle, but also brave and fearless. If you are to be humble, you cannot have one without the other.*

This is one of the great paradoxes of life: that inner strength is found in humility—a foreign concept in our world.

We find several biblical examples of this in men like John the Baptist, the apostle Paul and Moses. One of my favorite examples of true humility in a man comes from Numbers 12:3, where we learn Moses was the most humble man on the face of the earth. Yet, we see Moses go before the most powerful man on earth at the time—Pharaoh, king of Egypt—who could have easily had him killed.

Moses stood before Pharaoh, saying to him with great boldness, "I want you to let my people go. I want you to give up your entire slave labor force, the key to your entire economic and military superiority. I want you to do it quickly." (author's paraphrase of the story found in Exodus 5–12)

This polarity of characteristics you find in the truly humble–kind but fearless, gentle yet bold–is most clearly noted in the life of Jesus. In Revelation 5:5-6, Jesus is referred to as both a lion and a lamb. In Mathew 11, He refers to Himself as gentle and meek. He is, after all, the God of the universe who has restrained His power to become one of us.

Napoleon recognized this great paradox in the life of Jesus. At the end of his life, Napoleon made this observation:

> I die before my time and my body shall be given back to the earth and devoured by worms. What an abysmal gulf between my deep miseries and the eternal Kingdom of Christ. I marvel that whereas the ambitious dreams of myself and of Alexander and of Caesar should have vanished into thin air, a Judean peasant—Jesus—should be able to stretch His hands across the centuries and control the destinies of men and nations.

Here are three famous men—Alexander the Great, Caesar and Napoleon—seeking to control the world by power. When we see their lives contrasted with one man, Jesus, living the humble life of a carpenter, we marvel at how truly extraordinary He must have been to powerfully change the world through His simple life of humility.

The biblical understanding is that the humble are the strongest. They don't make decisions by sticking their fingers in the air to see what other people think. They have a fortitude, an inner strength that comes only through God's grace. They know who they are. Their lives are not consumed by trying to please and impress others.

Conversely, the arrogant feel as though they are superior to others and have this need to impress them. Although they believe themselves to be great and powerful, in reality, they are crippled with a sense of inferiority and insecurity. They are extremely needy. They need to feed their egos; they need compliments; they need to be stroked; they need to be recognized. Though they do not realize it, the proud are clearly weak, and this is what makes them ineffective as leaders.

5.5

What Gets You Up in the Morning?

AUTHOR TONY SCHWARTZ wrote a fascinating article in *The New York Times*, "What Gets You Up in the Morning?" He opens the article with this illuminating story:

> In the last several weeks, I had two radically different experiences spending extended time with leaders at two large global companies. A long, alcohol-fueled dinner with the first group was a pure downer: dull, rote and devoid of positive energy.
>
> The day with the second—a group of young managers at Google—was utterly exhilarating. After eight hours together, discussing what it takes to be an inspiring leader, the conversation was still going strong.
>
> What accounts for the difference?
>
> The Google leaders were considerably younger than their counterparts in the first group, who worked for a financial services company. Also, Google is regularly recognized as a great place to work. But, the most powerful difference, I'm convinced, is that the Googlers—hundreds of whom I've worked with over the years—feel they're contributing to something meaningful and larger than themselves, and the other executives evinced no passion whatsoever for their work.

Purpose is a uniquely powerful source of fuel—and satisfaction. That's why we resonate so strongly with exhortations that speak to it.

Further exemplifying the significance of purpose, the character Princeton sums it up lyrically in the musical "Avenue Q."

Purpose.
It's that little flame
that lights a fire
under your ass.
Purpose.
It keeps you going
like a car with a full
tank of gas.

Schwartz also adds:

Purpose is grounded in contribution, the sense we are headed in a clear direction, for a good reason. The Greeks call it "Telos"—one's ultimate goal, aim or intention.

Schwartz's words should challenge each of us into asking if our lives have a sense of purpose. Do I believe what I am doing with my life really matters?

He provides great insight into how to lead a purposeful life:

The most reliable sense of purpose, I'm convinced, is being of service to others—giving more than you take, which turns out not just to make most of us feel good, but also good about ourselves. In short, it's a powerful source of energy.

If you're a teacher, a social worker or a nurse, your work is intrinsically of service to others. But, there are many ways to be of service. Over the years, I've been inspired by parking lot attendants, shoe shiners, elevator operators, TSA agents and a smiling, upbeat clerk working in a Department of Motor Vehicles.

They'd found a way—whatever the intrinsic limitations of their job—to add value in the world, and to make meaning, one person at a time. We must not, in trying to think about how we can make a big difference, ignore the small daily differences we can make, which, over time, add up to the big differences we often cannot foresee.

We simply do not realize the significance of living and working with a sense of purpose.

In Copenhagen, there is an independent think tank, The Happiness Research Institute, that explores why some societies are happier than others. They recently surveyed 2,600 Danish workers from all types of industries to determine the sources of professional contentment. The clear winner was a "sense of purpose," which contributed twice as much to an individual's job satisfaction than all other factors. The study determined that we need a sense of purpose in our work.

Meik Wiking is the institution's CEO and notes that the Greek philosopher Aristotle recognized a close connection between happiness and a sense of purpose. He saw that our ultimate goal was not an easy life, but rather one filled with meaning, striving toward a goal.

Dr. Philip Pizzo, formerly the dean of Stanford's medical school and today the director of Stanford's Distinguished Career Institute, warns of the danger of drifting through your career without purpose. He believes it can be quite costly, stating there is a growing body of evidence demonstrating that a sense of purpose is a powerful predictor of mental and physical healthiness. He continues to add that those who report a strong sense of purpose are much less likely to die over a given period of time. They are far less likely to suffer a stroke or heart attack and less susceptible to viruses and certain cancers. Perhaps most significantly, Dr. Pizzo reveals that working and living with a sense of purpose can stave off one of the greatest terrors of every adult—Alzheimer's disease—stating:

Researchers at Rush University Medical Center have found that a third of people whose brains, upon autopsy, display the plaques and tangles of Alzheimer's never exhibited memory loss or intellectual impairment. The best predictor of whether someone would escape these symptoms was whether they felt strongly that they had a purpose in life. Those who did were two and a half times as likely to be unafflicted as those who didn't.

With so much at stake, we all should step back and examine our lives and careers. How do we view our work? What I have found is that, for most people, work is nothing more than a means to make money, support their families and hopefully, enable them to accumulate enough money to retire someday. However, their approach to work is very self-serving. It is all about them.

The purpose of work is not just about making money. It is about serving. It is to make ourselves available to others so we can serve them. When we make this our core objective, our work feels more purposeful. We find we enjoy it more. What I have witnessed is that when you serve your clients and customers with excellence, in all likelihood, you see your life and your business flourish.

In theory, this may sound quite good, but how do we make it a reality? We will consider that in the next essay.

5.6

Finding Purpose in Our Work

ONE OF THE wisest men I know once told me that a person's perspective is of critical importance because it impacts the way we see the world. It changes our priorities and the way we approach life. He told me if you want to see long-term change in a person's life, you must first change his or her perspective.

One of the world's great architects was a man by the name of Christopher Wren. He designed St. Paul's Cathedral in London, which was built between 1675 and 1710. During construction, everything was tirelessly performed by hundreds of workers since there were no machines or equipment to assist with their work.

One day, Wren was examining the job site, where the workers trudged away at their laborious task. There was nothing enjoyable about it.

Suddenly, Wren noticed an older man who was mixing cement in a mortar box. The man seemed to enjoy his work, wearing a smile on his face. As he watched this man mix the mortar, he finally asked him: "Mister, what are you doing?" The man replied, "Sir, I am building a great cathedral to the glory of God."

I am sure that most of the men working on the cathedral saw their work as drudgery and considered it as nothing more than a way to make a living. However, this older man had a completely different experience because of his perspective.

He saw himself engaged in a noble task of great significance, and it changed everything.

To find purpose in our work, sometimes you have to change your perspective. Dr. Tom Morris shares a great example of this in his book, *The Art of Achievement.* He tells the story of Nick Campbell, an engineer with Johnson & Johnson, who once found his work to be pure drudgery.

He worked entirely for himself, thinking only about what was good for his career. But, he was not getting the rewards or promotions he so desperately wanted. Every day was filled with frustration. He hated Monday mornings days in advance. Coworkers even called him "B.A." for "bad attitude."

When he was 29 years old, back surgery took Campbell out of the fray and gave him time to stop and think about his life, his attitudes and his mental approach to work. It was then that he realized what he had been doing was not working and that it had to change. Reading highly acclaimed business materials and motivational literature, he began to understand the role of attitude and inner visions for outer success. As a result, he used his imagination to envision his work in a whole new way, making an inner change that made more of a difference than he ever could have imagined.

Campbell began to think of himself as working for Campbell, Inc., a wholly owned "subsidiary" of Johnson & Johnson. He took emotional ownership of the equipment in the lab, checking it at the end of the day to ensure it was clean and ready for the next morning. He also saw himself as being in the customer service business, treating all of his associates as his customers. If he helped them solve their problems, he had a successful day.

He arrived to work each day with a completely new attitude of expectant challenge, helpfulness and emotional investment. And for the first time ever, he enjoyed his work. People soon thanked him for a job well done, and he experienced pride in each day's work. In the midst of these positive changes, Campbell was summoned to his supervisor's office. Initially, he worried he was being perceived as taking too much time from his primary assignments to help others solve problems. But, there was no cause for anxiety. Because of what he had accomplished for the whole department, and in recognition of his new level of commitment, Campbell was promoted two levels. The prize that had eluded him when he sought it directly was now being handed to him for serving his coworkers.

Campbell's life and career were transformed once he developed a new perspective, leading to more creative thinking and a new sense of purpose in his job.

Motivational speaker Barbara Glanz shared another wonderful story at an event, where she addressed 3,000 frontline workers for a large grocery store chain.

Glanz spoke of how people can make a difference, describing how every interaction with another person is a chance to create a memory—to bless someone's life. She emphasized how important it is to look for those moments.

After finishing her presentation, Glanz left her phone number, inviting conference attendees to call if they wanted to further discuss something she had said.

A month later, Glanz received a call from a 19-year-old bagger named Johnny. Johnny proudly informed her he had Down syndrome and then he told her his story.

"Barbara," Johnny said, "I liked what you talked about. But, I didn't think I could do anything special for our customers. After all I'm just a bagger."

After speaking to Glanz, Johnny had an idea. Every night when he came home from work, he would find a "thought for the day" for his next shift. It would be something positive, a reminder of how good it was to be alive, how people matter, or how many gifts surround us. If he could not find one, he would simply make one up.

Each night, his dad helped him enter the thought for the day six times on a page on the computer; then Johnny printed 50 pages, carefully cutting each page to create 300 sayings and signing every one.

Johnny put the stack of copies next to him while he worked. When he finished bagging someone's groceries, he placed a saying on top of the last bag. He then stopped what he was doing, looked the person straight in the eye, and said, "I've put a great saying in your bag. I hope it helps you have a good day. Thanks for coming here."

A month later, the store manager called Glanz. "You won't believe what's happened here," he told her. "I was making my rounds, and when I reached the cashiers, the line at Johnny's checkout was three times longer than anyone else's. It went all the way down the frozen food aisle!"

The manager announced on the loudspeaker that more checkout lines were open, but no customers moved. Instead, they patiently replied, "That's okay. We'll wait. We want to be in Johnny's line."

One woman took the manager's hand, saying, "I used to shop in your store once a week. Now, I come in every time I pass by—I want to get Johnny's thought for the day!" Johnny is doing more than filling bags with groceries; he is filling lives with hope.

You may have thought bagging groceries could not have been a vastly purposeful occupation. However, once Johnny realized he could bless and encourage others, a job that once seemed uninspiring became highly significant.

5.7

A Modern Business Parable

READING IN the book of Luke (12:15–21), there is a parable that carries enormous relevance to people in the sphere of business. Author John Ortberg retells this parable in a modern setting. Though he lengthens the story, he drives home the core truth that Jesus teaches.

There was a very successful man who owned a very successful business. Like many successful people, he was consumed with his work. He did what it took to get the job done. Even when he wasn't working, his mind would always drift back to the business.

His wife continually tries to get him to slow down, to spend more time at home with his family. He is vaguely aware that the kids are growing up, and he was missing it. However, the kids had come to the point of not expecting much from him.

He continually thinks to himself, "I will be more available next year when things settle down. He, however, never notices that things do not ever settle down.

He continually reminds himself and his wife, "I am doing it for you and the kids."

His wife urges him to go to church, and he goes on occasion, but he prefers to sleep in because it is the only day to do so. He would have more time for church when things settle down.

One night he feels a twinge of pain in his chest, and his wife rushes him to the hospital. He suffers a mild heart attack. His doctor informs him of the changes that he must make in his lifestyle. So, he cuts down on red meat and ice cream, and begins an exercise program. Soon, he feels much better and all the pain goes away. Eventually, he lets things slide, reminding himself that he will get in better shape when things settle down.

One day, the CFO of his company comes in to see him. He is told by the CFO that the business is booming to the point that "we cannot keep up with all of the orders. We have the chance to strike the 'mother lode.' If we can catch this wave, we can all be set for life. However, we need larger facilities, new equipment, and the new state-of-the-art technology and delivery systems to keep up with all of our orders."

So, the man becomes more consumed with his work, every waking moment is devoted to this once-in-a-lifetime opportunity.

He tells his wife, "You know what this means, don't you? When I am through with this new phase, I will be able to relax. We will be set for life. I have covered all the bases, prepared for every contingency. We will be financially secure and can finally take all those trips you have been wanting to go on." She, of course, has heard this before, and so she does not get her hopes up.

At about 11:00 that night, she tells her husband she is going to bed and asks him if he is ready to go up with her. "You go ahead," he tells her. "I will be up in a minute. I have one thing I want to finish on the computer."

She goes upstairs, falls asleep, and wakes up at 3 a.m. She realizes her husband is not in bed and heads downstairs, finding him asleep at the computer. She reaches out to wake him, but his skin is cold. He does not respond. She gets a sick feeling in the pit of her stomach and dials 911.

When the paramedics arrive, they tell her he died of a massive heart attack some hours ago.

His death is the major item of discussion in the financial community. His extensive obituary is written up in all of the newspapers. It is a shame he was dead, for he would have loved to have read all the good things written about him.

They have a memorial service and because of his prominence, the whole community comes out for it. Several people get up to eulogize him at the service. One says, "He was one of the leading entrepreneurs of the day. He was a real leader." Another says, "He was a real innovator in new technology and delivery systems." A third says, "He was a man of principles, would never cheat anyone." It was noted by many that he was a pillar in the community and was known and liked by everyone. His life was truly a success.

Then they buried him, and they all went home. Later that night in the cemetery, an angel of God makes his way through the markers and tombstones. He stands before this man's memorial tombstone and tracks with his finger the single word God has chosen to summarize this man's life. If you are familiar with the parable, you know the word. "Fool."

Listen to Jesus' simple and direct conclusion to the parable in Luke 12:20–21:

> You fool! This very night your soul is required of you, and now who will own what you have prepared? So is the man who lays up treasure for himself, and is not rich toward God" (and the things of God).

This makes me realize that my greatest fear should never be fear of failure, but the fear of investing my entire life in something that does not really matter.

6

FINANCIAL WISDOM

*The great part of the miseries of mankind is brought upon them by
false estimates they have made of the value of things.*

~ Ben Franklin

6.1

Wisdom and the Building of Wealth

O NE OF THE best books ever written on personal finance, in my opinion, is *The Millionaire Next Door,* by Dr. Thomas Stanley and Dr. William Danko. It was published more than 20 years ago, making its millionaire of the past worth around $2 million to $3 million today. The book opens with an intriguing scenario:

These people cannot be millionaires! They don't look like millionaires, they don't dress like millionaires, they don't eat like millionaires, they don't act like millionaires–they don't even have millionaire names. Where are the millionaires who look like millionaires?

The person who said this was a vice president of a trust department. He made these comments following a focus group interview and dinner that we hosted for 10 first-generation millionaires. His view of millionaires is shared by most people who are not wealthy. They think millionaires own expensive clothes, watches and other status artifacts. We have found this not to be the case.

As a matter of fact, our trust officer friend spends significantly more for his suits than the typical American millionaire. He also wears a $5,000 watch. We know from our surveys that the majority of millionaires never spent even one-tenth of

$5,000 for a watch. Our friend also drives a current-model imported luxury car. Most millionaires are not driving this year's model. Only a minority drive a foreign motor vehicle. An even smaller minority drive foreign luxury cars. Our trust officer leases, while only a minority of millionaires ever lease their motor vehicles.

But, ask the typical American adult this question: Who looks more like a millionaire? Would it be our friend, the trust officer, or one of the people who participated in our interview? We would wager that most people by a wide margin would pick the trust officer. But, looks can be deceiving.

Drs. Stanley and Danko spent 20 years studying the lives of the affluent before they published their findings. They began by surveying those who lived in upscale neighborhoods throughout the country. Over time, they discovered many of the people who live in expensive homes and drive fancy cars do not have much wealth. Even so, many people who do have a great deal of wealth do not live in upscale neighborhoods.

The researchers recognized that people have allowed themselves to be deceived. They have it all wrong about building wealth, as having a big income is not the same as being wealthy. If a family has a large income, but spends it all every year, they are not building wealth. They are living lavishly. People can have a hard time understanding that wealth is what you accumulate, not what you spend.

The most perplexing question in my mind is, "How is it that so many people who make a great deal of money and live lavish lifestyles are flat broke?" They have little or no net worth other than maybe the equity in their homes. What would cause someone to live so foolishly and not make better decisions? Undoubtedly, just about everyone likes nice things and could enjoy a high-end lifestyle, but there is a deeper issue involved that you may not be aware of.

In 1899, economist Thorstein Veblen wrote the book, "The Theory of the Leisure Class." Veblen coined a special term describing many upper-income Americans.

Conspicuous Consumption

This is when you buy something, not primarily for its usefulness, but for the way it makes you look in the eyes of others. Veblen shared the following message in 1899:

> People above the line of base subsistence, in this age and all ear-lier ages, do not use the surplus, which society has given them, primarily for useful purposes. They do not seek to expand their own lives, to live more wisely, intelligently, understandingly, but to impress other people with the fact that they have a surplus... spending money, time and effort quite uselessly in the pleasur-able business of inflating the ego.

Though we may not realize it, there is a psychological fulfillment which comes from being envied by others. Veblen contended that it is possible to persuade people to buy products that are not particu-larly superior in quality by publicizing widely that the products are expensive.

This is how he came up with the term *conspicuous consumption*. People buy costly items, not because they are higher quality, but be-cause the possession displays to others how rich the owners are.

Veblen expresses that we often make purchases to make a statement to the world that we are wealthy. Furthermore, in this modern culture of easy credit, men and women accumulate enormous debt just to live lavishly and "keep up with the Joneses."

It is amazing how we allow the opinions of others to influence the decisions we make and how we choose to live our lives. This illustrates how people with high incomes can become conspicuous consumers and have little to show for it at the end of the day.

6.2

Solomon's Insight on Money and Wealth

NUMEROUS INDIVIDUALS would contend that King Solomon was the richest person to ever live, exhibiting staggering wealth. As one commentator put it, "Solomon made Bill Gates look like a second-class citizen."

Solomon's philosophical writings in the book of Ecclesiastes offer fascinating perspectives on money, particularly when you consider how much wealth he had.

First, he reflects on the day he will have to leave all the fruit of his labor to someone else, asking: "Who knows whether he will be a wise man or a fool?" (Ecclesiastes 2:19)

Solomon laments the notion that eventually someone else will have total control over the wealth that resulted from his own labor and toil. This thought left him in great despair.

An interesting article was published in the June 17, 2015 edition of *Time* magazine titled, "70% of Rich Families Lose Their Wealth by the Second Generation." The article highlights how poorly prepared the second generation is at handling the wealth that is passed down to it. As one financial consultant put it, "Most of them have no clue as to the value of money . . ." The article also points out that the third generation is usually financially doomed.

Knowing this, you can see why Solomon found the thought of leaving his hard-earned estate to someone who would squander it to be so depressing. Which leads to Solomon's second perspective on money:

"Whoever loves money never has enough" (Ecclesiastes 5:10)

This seems to be a natural part of the human condition. There is never enough; we always want more.

Ron Blue is a Christian financial consultant and has supported a missionary organization in Africa that works with people living in abject poverty. One year, Blue visited one of the missionaries to observe his work, asking the question, "What is the greatest barrier among these people that keeps you from reaching them with the gospel? Without hesitation, the missionary responded, "Materialism."

Blue was dumbfounded, as all he could see was extreme impoverishment. "How can that be?" Blue asked.

The missionary replied, "If a man has a manure hut, he wants a mud hut. If he has a mud hut, he wants a stone hut. If his hut has a thatched roof, he wants a tin roof. If he has one cow, he wants two cows. If he has one wife, he wants two wives, and so on and so on."

Blue recognized, as did Solomon, that materialism is not about things. It is about the heart and the insatiable desire for more.

Solomon made a third observation about wealth, stating, "Whoever loves wealth is never satisfied with his income." (Ecclesiastes 5:10) In other words, the fruit of our labor does not satisfy us. It does not fill the emptiness of life.

A perfect example that proves this theory involves studies that have been conducted on people who win lotteries. The winners always experience a huge surge of euphoria when they learn of their winnings. However, in almost every situation, within six months, those same people return to the same level of satisfaction they experienced before the lottery win.

I am sure you may be thinking you would be an exception to the rule, but consider this:

Money and wealth cannot purchase a:

1. *Good marriage*
2. *Meaningful family life*

3. *Friendship*
4. *Wisdom*
5. *Peace and contentment in your soul*

Finally, it cannot purchase the forgiveness of your sins and eternal life.

The bottom line is this—money and wealth cannot purchase the *true* riches of life.

6.3

The Root of
Financial Problems

S EVERAL YEARS AGO, I performed a study on money and finance,
and ran across some noteworthy remarks by King David:

> He has dug a pit and hollowed it out, and has fallen into the hole,
> which he made." (Psalm 7:15)

This is what often happens to people with their finances. They dig a
deep financial hole, generally because they incur too much debt, and
then they fall in the hole.

In the book of Proverbs, we read where the wise person under-
stands his ways and carefully considers his steps, particularly as they
relate to finances. (Proverbs 14:8,15) On the other hand, a fool is one
who is out of touch with reality. They are not forward thinking and
therefore, do not give much thought to financial planning, running up
large amounts of debt instead.

Not long ago, a young man visited my office, seeking advice. Though
I didn't know him very well, he appeared to be successful based on the
upscale neighborhood he lived in and the lifestyle he led.

I quickly learned that his marriage was in trouble, and he was
experiencing incredible financial pressure. He had maxed out all
lines of credit, had no equity in his house, and was struggling just
to pay the mortgage. Finally, he told me that selling his house and

downsizing was not an option, because his wife refused to move out of their popular neighborhood.

I could not help him, because he was not in touch with reality. Over a 10-year period, he had dug a financial hole, fallen into it and did not know how to get out. It struck me how money has such a deceptive power. It blinds us in such a way that we make terrible financial decisions.

I find most financial problems to be the result of too much debt. Solomon addresses debt in the book of Proverbs.

The rich rules over the poor, and the borrower becomes the lender's slave. (Proverbs 22:7)

Do not be among those who give pledges, among those who become guarantors for debts. If you have nothing with which to pay, why should he take your bed from under you? (Proverbs 22:26,27)

I feel it is clear that debt is not sinful, but the Bible discourages it when it is not necessary. The main reason is because lenders have power over the borrower. I remember a very wise older man once said to me, "If you don't go into debt, you will never go bankrupt."

A good question we should consider is, "When is it wise to go into debt and when is it not? What is a good reason to go into debt and what is not?"

A majority of financial advisors would agree that a mortgage on your house or a loan on an automobile is reasonable, because the loan is backed by an asset that can be disposed of rather quickly to pay it off.

Sound bankers make good loans that make sense, and they do it to protect the bank, while protecting the borrower, as well. It is when lending institutions throw their standards out the window that they get in trouble, as do the borrowers. This is what happened in this last financial crisis.

Greg Brenneman is one of the world's leading business turnaround executives. In his book, *Right Away and All at Once,* he shares wise words on debt. He says we should always match our debts with the life of our asset. There is a reason that your credit card bills come due every 30 days, your car loan in five years, and most home mortgages in 30 years. These loans have been set up to match the life of the underlying asset. Groceries and a tank of gasoline last less than a month, automobiles last five years or more, and homes much longer.

Where people get in trouble is when they borrow to support lavish lifestyles through items such as jewelry, designer clothes and vacations. This is generally done with credit card debt, and when this happens, it is the beginning of digging a hole.

Michael Kidwell and Steve Rhode, authors of *Get Out of Debt: Smart Solutions to Your Money Problems*, share this:

> *Debt is one of the leading causes of divorce, lack of sleep and poor work performance. It is truly one of the deep, dark secrets that people have. It robs them of their self-worth and keeps them from achieving dreams.*

The Bible does not have many suggested financial goals, but it does appear to teach that being debt-free is a wise objective. When a person is out of debt, he or she discovers their possessions and lifestyle no longer possess them.

6.4

The Danger of an Easy Life

SEVERAL YEARS AGO, *Fortune* magazine featured a special edition titled, "Retire Early and Rich." You see this type of theme often in financial magazines. They know what sells magazines and are certainly aware that the number one goal of middle- and upper-class workers is early retirement.

Americans from all walks of life yearn for an easy, carefree life with no worries or stress. It's a good life that we all dream to achieve. Often, we refer to this as the American Dream.

Author and businessman Bob Buford warns us to be careful with the idea that the object of work is to earn enough money so we can lead a life of leisure. He calls it, "living in leisure world," the life you thought you always wanted.

Buford conveys a powerful story to make a point of how life in leisure world can be exceedingly dangerous:

> Rogers Kirven was about to cash out his successful business. It would have given him enough money so that he would never have to work again for the rest of his life. Rogers had worked extremely hard to get to this enviable position, and he wanted to reward himself. He envisioned the life of his dreams: more time with his wife and family, never having to start each day with a trip to the office, and most of all, freedom.

The day was almost there when all he had to do was sign his name and he would have enough cash to do whatever he wanted for the rest of his life. For some reason, just before he was to close the deal, he decided to celebrate with two longtime buddies who had sold their companies a few years earlier. They met at a restaurant in Washington, D.C., and very soon into the conversation, Rogers began to get nervous.

"The first thing they told me was that they had new wives," Kirven said. "I'd known one of them for 15 years; the other for seven years. Both of them had cashed out to spend more time with their families!"

The conversation never got much beyond their toys and leisure activities, and the more they talked, the more terrified Rogers became. Instead of being excited about their lives, they seemed confused and disconnected, still wondering what to do with their lives. "There was a creeping sensation of 'Uh oh! Something has happened to my friends,'" Kirven said.

On the way out of the restaurant, Rogers was still looking for confirmation from them that cashing out to leisure world was the best thing they had ever done. But, when he asked one of the guys that exact question, all he got in return was, "I don't know. I don't know."

Rogers decided to track down every person he could find who, in search of a better life, had cashed in seeking relief from "first half pressures." When last I talked to him, he had interviewed 36 men between the ages of 40 and 50, who had turned their businesses into at least $45 million. This certainly isn't a statistically projectable sample, but I find it at the very least, an interesting and instructive window into the American Dream. How did it turn out?

"The first three guys I talked to were just like me," Rogers told me. "They loved God, loved their families, and were in the same age bracket, 42–44. They all had a strategy. They wanted to spend more time with their families and develop their own souls.

"Within a year, all three were divorced. All three blew at least $1 million on new toys—bigger boat, bigger car, bigger plane.

They all thought they had a solid game plan, but like Mike Tyson said about his boxing foes, 'They all had a strategy until they got hit.' Each of these guys stepped into a stream, and they didn't realize the current was so strong until they got swept away."

Of the 36 guys he interviewed, a remarkable 32 got divorced! All of them locked their targets on a new toy or affair, but experienced tremendous depression after "acquiring" each new thing. What seemed like paradise turned out to be just the opposite. These guys tried what most of us would say is the ideal arrangement. Money is no object. You don't have to go to work. You can travel, play and buy all you want. And instead of waiting until these guys were too old to enjoy their freedom, they did it while they were quite young. Somehow, it just didn't pan out the way they thought it would.

Kirven was lucky in that he swerved from leisure world at the last minute. He concluded work is healthier than you think.

God clearly made us to be productive and, therefore, we should not just sell our businesses or retire and go to leisure world, but find new work that adds meaning and purpose to our life. I heard someone say that we should be like Tarzan. He never let go of the vine he was swinging on until he clearly had his hand firmly affixed on the next one.

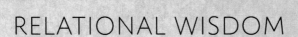

7

RELATIONAL WISDOM

I know of no more potent killer than isolation. There is no more destructive influence on physical and mental health than the isolation of you from me and us from them.
— Dr. Philip Zimbardo

7.1

Relational Beings

IN THE LATE 1930's, a group of 268 young men, including John F. Kennedy and Ben Bradlee (who would later become editor of *The Washington Post*), entered Harvard University as freshmen. They were highly intelligent, affluent and ambitious as they joined the freshman class of one of the world's most highly acclaimed universities.

Yet, these were no ordinary Harvard men. This specially chosen group was subject to one of the century's most fascinating longitudinal studies. They were offered and accepted into an academic study as sophomores to be observed. Today, members still living have been studied for more than 70 years. Results from the study, known as The Grant Study, have become well known across the world in our pursuit to understand what makes us happy.

As some of our best and brightest men of their time, these men suffered from various issues including alcoholism, depression and broken families. After sifting through the data and research on their lives, George Vaillant, who oversaw the study for decades, concluded that healthy relationships with family and friends are the single most important variable that contributes to our happiness.

This should be of no surprise, as God clearly made us to be relational beings. We know this is true because, if we were not relational beings, there would be no loneliness. Crippling loneliness plagues our land, particularly in the lives of men who struggle being transparent with anyone.

Author Donald Miller reveals:

> . . . the words alone, lonely and loneliness are three of the most powerful words in the English language. Those words say we are human; they are like the words hunger and thirst. But, they are not words about the body, but the soul."
>
> "I think it is interesting that God designed people to need other people."
>
> "Our souls need to interact with other people to be healthy.

Not only do we need intimate relationships to be vibrant and healthy, we also need them to survive. An experiment in the 16th century demonstrates this point.

King Frederick (1712–1786) arranged for several babies to be segregated at birth. They were neither talked to nor cuddled, but nurses made sure their physical needs were met. Frederick's intention was to discover what the true language of humanity was and he eventually found his answer, though it was tragic for the little children. All of the babies used in the experiment died. They literally died from lack of love.

Many modern social scientists believe our relationships are deteriorating in the wake of social media. Even when you consider all of the online social networks now available, they cannot replace authentic human connections. The research is utterly clear that this increased connectivity on social media is leading to greater loneliness.

Clearly, we are relational beings who need to love and be loved. Everything that isolates and separates us from meaningful relationships is harmful to our well-being.

Therefore, if the relationships with our family and friends are our most priceless assets, what are we doing to protect them? And what are we doing to nourish them? We must be deeply intentional in the pursuit of quality time with the people God has placed in our lives, knowing that the deeper and more intimate our relationships, the richer our lives will be.

7.2

Thoughts About Marriage

I WATCH MANY couples struggle in their marriages. And I see many of them end in divorce.

Think back to when you first met your spouse, when you began to date, fall in love, and then become engaged. It was likely one of the most wonderful times of your entire life. One of the main reasons this is true is because the major component of what you were experiencing was based on physical attraction and romantic love. Sparks and electricity light up the room every time you see your new love. There is no room to detect flaws in the person. As the old cliché goes, love is blind.

Once you are married and time goes by, the sparks turn to flickering embers, charm fades and you are left with the person. At this point, you begin to realize the love you have for your spouse is not based on physical attraction. It is the person you love, particularly his or her heart.

This is why, whenever I am asked to participate in a wedding ceremony or give pre-marital counsel, I emphasize the importance of spiritual life and the need to grow spiritually. I explain to each couple that, as you deepen your relationship with Christ, He will transform your heart, and this will draw you into a deeper love, because you are drawn to each other's heart.

My second thought about marriage is that we often make the colossal mistake of looking to our spouse to provide something that only God can provide. Nowadays, men and women look to their spouse and unconsciously declare, "I am looking to you to make me happy." Lots of people enter marriage this way and, in the process, expect too much from the relationship.

When we look to Christ to satisfy the deep longing of our souls, we approach marriage with the right perspective. And we are not placing the pressure on our spouse to do what only Jesus can do. Gary Thomas articulates this beautifully in his thoughtful book, *Sacred Marriage.*

> It is common to enter marriage with the belief that my spouse is going to make me happy—but, over time we realize that the ideal relationship we had always dreamed of does not come to pass. Thus, we become disillusioned by the inability to receive all the love we believe we should be getting from our spouses. Of course, in this culture in which we live, the most popular option in dealing with this disillusionment is to look for a new relationship. We rationalize within ourselves and reason that "I just need to find the right person," which translated usually means a new person. However, in a new relationship, the same process will inevitably repeat itself—great excitement, the thrill of discovery, and then at some point, disillusionment. A new person might look new for a couple of years, and she might be a little shinier with a few less wrinkles, but eventually, we discover that she has so many of the same limitations as the person we traded in.
>
> What we fail to realize is that God must be at the center of our hearts, and all of our other relationships should flow out of that one central relationship. As odd as this may sound, I have discovered in my own life that my satisfaction or dissatisfaction with my marriage has far more to do with my relationship with God than it does my relationship with my wife. Therefore, we should never blame our spouse for our lack of fulfillment; we should blame ourselves for not more diligently pursuing a ful-filling relationship with God.

7.3

Thoughts About Marriage, Part 2

T HE NATURAL TENDENCY of everything in life is to move from order to disorder. At some point during the formal education of most Americans, this concept of *entropy* was taught and learned. Everything in your life that is not protected and nurtured deteriorates. This includes your car, your house and your clothes. Therefore, if you want to see any area of your life deteriorate, do nothing.

This is particularly true in marriage. It is easy for a man to drift slowly away from his spouse and not realize it.

Ned Holstein is the executive director of National Parents Organization, a nonprofit also known as Fathers and Families until 2013. Holstein says, "Most men think that they are safe because they are good husbands, fathers and providers. But, most divorces are sought by women, and many men have no idea that a divorce is coming."

For you men reading this book, ask yourself, "Could this possibly be happening in my marriage?" Maybe we should open our eyes and take a long hard look at our relationship with our wives.

What I have repeatedly seen is that many men neglect their wives and are not even aware of it. Wives handle this neglect in one of two ways. Some will confront it, often out of anger and frustration, but at least their husbands know something's wrong. However, others respond by saying nothing. They go silent. They might hint at their dissatisfaction, but their husbands do not get it. In the process, their marriage slowly dies, and the husband only becomes aware of it when she files for divorce. I have seen it happen many times.

A second thought involves the real path that leads to discovering true happiness in your marriage. Dr. Tim Keller delivers interesting insight concerning this topic:

> The Bible says that human beings were made in God's image. That means, among other things, that we were created to worship and live for God's glory, not our own. We were made to serve God and others. That means, paradoxically, that if we try to put our own happiness ahead of obedience to God, we violate our own nature and become, ultimately, miserable. Jesus restates the principle when he says, "Whoever wants to save his life shall lose it, but whoever loses his life for my sake will find it." (Matthew 16:25) He is saying, "If you seek happiness more than you seek me, you will have neither; if you seek to serve me more than you serve your own quest for happiness, you will have both.

> Paul applies this principle to marriage. Seek to serve one another rather than to be happy, and you will find a new and deeper happiness. Many couples have discovered this wonderful, unlooked-for reality. Why would this be true? It is because it is "instituted of God." It was established by the God for whom self-giving love is an essential attribute, and therefore it reflects His nature, particularly as it is revealed in the person and work of Jesus Christ.

Christian apologist C. S. Lewis believes this to be one of the most significant universal principles in all of life: "Give up yourself and you will find your real self."

Another way to approach this is to view marriage as if you are joining the military. When you join the military, you lose control over your schedule, when you take a holiday, when you eat your meals, etc. You ultimately surrender your independence and the freedom to make unilateral choices. In the process, you become part of a whole; you become part of a greater unity.

This, of course, is not instinctive and initially you will find it to be unnatural. But, this is the very foundation of marriage. It is necessary if you are going to experience true oneness.

7.4

Saving Your Marriage

WHEN MARRIAGE GETS tough, it does not mean it is time to throw in the towel. Author Philip Yancey shares valuable insight on the difficulty of marriage.

> *Every marriage has crisis times, moments of truth when one partner (or both) is tempted to give up, to judge the other undependable, irrational, untrustworthy. Great marriages survive these weak moments; weak ones fall apart. When divorce happens, tragically, both partners lose out on the deeper strength that comes only from riding out such stormy times together. Great relationships take form when they are stretched to the breaking point and do not break.*

Through the years, I have shared Yancey's words with couples struggling in their marriages. For the stronger ones, it re-energized them, giving them hope. For others, you could tell, they had already given up. They had somehow concluded that, since the passion was gone and their feelings had died, there was no reason to keep the marriage together. Instead of trying to fight for their marriage, they were ready to move on and look for a new relationship.

In the early years of Christendom, the medieval church established a list of seven deadly sins. These were considered to be evil dispositions that motivated us toward destructive behaviors. Many people are surprised when they hear that the first of these sins is "sloth" or what we would call "laziness." But, is sloth really that harmful?

Dr. Scott Peck, an American psychiatrist who has written some of the most popular books in psychotherapy, believes laziness is a major cause of evil, a primary cause of psychological illness, and the main reason Americans are increasingly failing in their relationships, particularly marriage.

Essentially, to love someone, you need not be lazy. Love requires commitment and work. It requires effort, regardless of how you feel.

Dr. Tim Keller adds:

Nearly everyone thinks that the Bible's directive to "love your neighbor" is wise, right and good. But, notice that it is a command, and emotions cannot be commanded. The Bible does not call us to like our neighbor, to have affection and warm feelings toward him or her. No, the call is to love your neighbor, and that must primarily mean displaying a set of behaviors.

We know feelings are real, but they are not reliable. Feelings are not consistent and are tied to a number of complex factors, waxing and waning. Dr. Keller makes a solid point in that our emotions are not always under our control, but our actions are.

I know of a counselor who strongly believes that feelings of love will follow acts of love. When he counsels those who are struggling in their marriage, he lays out a challenge for them, asking for a four-week commitment. Every day for the next four weeks, they are to do five things each day that someone in love would do. The first thing each morning, they are to make a list of five specific things to do for the other person to express love.

The results? Invariably, over that four-week period, couples begin to see real progress. Unfortunately, most spouses refuse to accept this challenge because they do not think that they are responsible for their marital problems. In reality, they are too lazy to put forth the effort to love their spouse, seeing divorce as an easier alternative.

As you examine your marriage today, are you truly loving your spouse through your actions? Christian author C. S. Lewis strongly believed that, even if you have feelings of indifference toward the one you love, you can change your heart over the long haul through your actions.

7.5

Thoughts on Marital Conflict

I N A MARRIAGE, conflict can manifest itself on various levels of complexity. Some conflicts are singular and can be resolved easily, while others become lost within a black hole, leading to divorce.

I have two concepts to consider when addressing marital conflict, with my first thought reflected in a post by Dr. Tim Keller:

> When I was a young pastor in a small Southern town, I did a lot of marriage counseling. Some marriages were harmed by things like drink, drugs, pornography or an extramarital affair. But, in most of the troubled marriages I saw, the problem stemmed not from bad things but from very good things that had become too important. When some good thing becomes more engrossing and important than your spouse, it can destroy the marriage.

He goes on to mention that if your spouse does not feel you are putting him or her first, then by definition, you are not. When this happens, your marriage is dying.

According to Dr. Keller, there are four primary "good things" we overcommit to in marital conflict.

The first and most obvious is our children. A strong marriage between husband and wife makes children grow up feeling the world is a safe place and love is possible. It is healthy for children to see that the marriage comes first.

On the other hand, take a look a mother who puts her children above her husband. It not only harms the marriage, but the children do not get to see how a good marriage works. By putting her children before her husband, she does not realize she is harming the children.

The second good thing is our parents. Some people never leave their parents. We are told to "Leave our fathers and mothers and cleave to our spouse." Often, people don't leave their parents and allow them to become too involved in their lives.

The third good thing is work. This is highly common in this age, where people are driven to be successful. If one spouse perceives that work is more important than the marriage, the relationship will slowly die.

The final good thing is our hobbies. If a spouse truly believes that a hobby is more important than the marriage, the relationship is in real trouble.

My second thought on marital conflict has to do with blame. When a marriage is in trouble, it is easy for spouses to point the finger at each other. They generally acknowledge they are partly to blame, but the real problem is their spouse.

Jesus gives thoughtful insight regarding this issue in the Sermon on the Mount:

> And why do you look at the speck that is in your brother's eye, but do not notice the log that is in your own eye? Or how can you say to your brother 'Let me take the speck out of your eye,' and behold, the log is in your own eye? You hypocrite, first take the log out of your own eye, and then you will see clearly to take the speck out of your brother's eye." (Mathew 7:3-5)

Jesus is telling us that we have a propensity to easily point out the flaws in the lives of others, when we are so blind to the major short-comings in our own lives. This is particularly true in marriage.

Author Gary Thomas has this to add:

> "I have a theory, behind virtually every case of marital dissatisfaction lies an unwillingness to admit our self-centeredness. Couples do not fall out of love so much as they are unwilling to humbly

acknowledge they have shortcomings as a spouse. Sin, wrong at-
titude and personal failures that are not dealt with slowly erode
the relationship, assaulting and, eventually, erasing the once lofty
promise in the throes of an earlier and less polluted love."

In essence, Jesus is telling us that, if we take responsibility for and
deal with our own selfishness, we are able to see the other person more
clearly, while being more effective in their lives.

It is essential to get a husband and a wife to stop blaming and pointing their fingers at each other and have each of them honestly answer
this question:

What am I doing to cause problems in this marriage?

Couples who are both willing to take this approach have a great opportunity to turn their marriage around and see it begin to grow and
flourish.

7.6

Being Intentional in Marriage

IN THE PAST few years, my wife and I have attended two beautiful weddings. Each bride and groom was from a loving family, and both weddings exemplified the joy of marital bliss. The weddings also shared a commonality we see all too often. Both marriages ended in divorce within only two years.

I have no doubt that, on their wedding day, each couple had high hopes and dreams for their future. Their intentions were good. But without realizing it, they chose a path that led to the demise of their marriages.

It is easy to believe that great marriages just happen because of the momentum of the romantic love that people share. However, in reality, if you want your marriage to grow and deepen in love and intimacy, you have to be intentional. It is essential to nurture the relationship, be proactive in demonstrating your love for your spouse, and look for ways to be creative. Spouses must also be vigilant in looking for unhealthy patterns they see developing.

Here are several ideas that have genuinely helped our marriage:

1. Do not be afraid to go for counselling. This is something my wife pushed in our early years of marriage and it has been invaluable.
2. Set aside time to be alone with your spouse, particularly when you are raising your children. This has to be planned. Many couples have arranged consistent date nights. Every year on our

anniversary, we get away for four or five days to be together and celebrate our marriage. During this time, we reminisce about our life together over the years.

3. Seek the wisdom of couples who are farther down the road in their marriages than you. This can be incredibly helpful.

4. Read good books on marriage. I highly recommend Gary Thomas' *Sacred Marriage,* Gary Chapman's *The Five Love Languages,* and Tim Keller's *The Meaning of Marriage.*

Finally, I leave you with a thought that has been vastly meaningful to me personally. Marriage is a covenant relationship. In the sight of God, it is a binding agreement. This is why you make vows to your spouse. The marriage vows are not about how much you love your spouse on the wedding day, it is a commitment of how you are going to love them in the future. In a covenant relationship, unless there are biblical grounds, divorce is not an option.

My wife and I have two dear friends whose marriage and advice have been a huge encouragement to us. They have been married 15 years longer than we have.

Early in their marriage, he was a surgical resident and they were living in another part of the country, far away from home. He was at the hospital almost every waking hour, and she was at home with their first two children. Their marriage was in a downward spiral, to the point they had great contempt for one another. I think she was ready to throw in the towel, pack her bags and head back home.

They finally reached a crossroads, and they realized personally, as Christians, divorce was not an option for them. They had no good reason to get divorced. That realization changed everything. They then began the long hard process of rebuilding their marriage. Here we are 30 years later, and they have a strong, solid marriage and a wonderful family.

As Philip Yancey says, "I wonder how many couples lose out on the deeper strength that comes only from riding out such stormy times together."

One of Life's Great Blessings: Friendship

ONE OF LIFE'S great blessings is friendship, and yet in this frenetic, technological world we live in, people do not appear to value it anymore. Particularly men.

Former NFL defensive lineman and motivational speaker Joe Ehrmann observes that men are constantly comparing and competing, wondering how they measure up to other men. It leaves them with feelings of isolation and loneliness. Coach Ehrmann mentions a study he read, revealing a sad fact: most men over the age of 35 have **no** authentic friends. That is, someone close to them with whom they can be vulnerable and share their innermost thoughts and feelings.

In his book, *The Question of God*, Armond Nicholi Jr., discusses C. S. Lewis' view of friendship. For years, Lewis was an atheist, exhibited a pessimistic view of life, and had zero friends. Yet, when he became a Christian, his view of life and relationships was transformed. As Nicholi put it, nothing brought Lewis more enjoyment than sitting around a fire with a group of close friends engaged in good conversation, or taking long walks through the English countryside, accompanied by a friend.

"My happiest hours," Lewis wrote, "are spent with three or four old friends in old clothes tramping together and putting up in small pubs—or else sitting up 'til the small hours in someone's college rooms, talking nonsense, poetry, theology, metaphysics . . . There's no sound I like better than . . . laughter."

In another letter to his good friend, Greeves, Lewis writes, "Friendship is the greatest of worldly goods. Certainly to me, it is the chief happiness of life. If I had to give a piece of advice to a young man about a place to live, I think I should say, 'sacrifice almost everything you have to live where you can be near your friends.'

Lewis changed from a wary introvert with very few close relationships to a personable extrovert with scores of close friends and colleagues. George Sayer, a biographer who knew Lewis for some 30 years, and Owen Barfield, a close friend for more than 40 years, described Lewis after his conversion.

"He was unusually cheerful, and took an almost boyish delight in life," they said, describing him as "great fun, an extremely witty and amusing companion . . . considerate. . . more concerned with the welfare of his friends than with himself."

Lewis clearly understood the value of friendship and was a loyal friend to others, as this was such a high priority in his life.

When you read the book of Proverbs, notice there are several verses on being a friend. It declares you will never be a wise person unless you are able to choose, develop and keep great friends.

Dr. Tim Keller says friendship can bring something into your life that neither your wife nor children can bring. The reason is that friendship is not of biological or sociological necessity. It is the only love that is absolutely deliberate, never pushing itself on you like a family does.

What you find is that, in a busy frenetic culture, good friendships are squeezed out. In fact, the book of Proverbs is clear, you will not have the life God wants for you without good friends.

Dr. Keller also reveals that friendships today are much more difficult to come by, because we are such a highly mobile society. We have less time to forge friendships. People move frequently, are traveling for business or pleasure, and have second and third homes. Without realizing it, modern people relegate friendship to a place of low priority.

There is no doubt in my mind that friendships have to be pursued. A wise rule to remember is that to have good friends you have to be a good friend. You have to be transparent and willing to speak honestly into someone else's life.

8

HUMAN SEXUALITY

*Human sexuality has never been more studied and pandered
to in public, yet we have never been more confused about what is
right, good, and beautiful!*
- *Ravi Zacharias*

8.1

The Purpose of
Our Sexuality

G EORGE LEONARD (1923–2010) was an American author and educator who wrote 15 books and served as the editor for *Look* magazine. For a number of years, Leonard was a big proponent of the sexual liberation movement, believing in complete sexual freedom—that one should enjoy sex with multiple partners.

To the dismay of some loyal followers, Leonard changed his direction years later, writing a book ironically titled, *The End of Sex: Erotic Love after the Sexual Revolution,* offering newly discovered insight.

"I have finally come to see that every game has a rule," Leonard said, "and sex has rules. Unless you play by the rules, you'll find sex can create a depth of loneliness that nothing else can."

If Leonard's observation is correct, that sex has rules and ignoring these rules leads to painful consequences, one must ask two simple questions: What are the rules and who makes them?

Clearly, sex was God's idea, but what did He have in mind when He gave us our sexuality? It only seems logical that, if our sexuality was God's idea, He must have a blueprint that leads to the ultimate sexual experience.

In the Old Testament, when a man has sex with his wife, the English translation generally is, "he lays with her." But, the actual Hebrew word for sex in the text is *yada.* In English, *yada* is shorthand for "boring, empty talk." But in Hebrew, it is a verb of action that means "to know, to be known, to be deeply respected." In fact, it sounds like a synonym for the best definition of intimacy. Using the Hebrew definition, sexual intercourse is not just for pleasure, but its function or purpose is to know or be deeply known by someone.

There is also a frequently used Hebrew word that is parallel to *yada*, and it is the word *hessed*, meaning "deep friendship and loyalty." Clearly, God designed sex so that two people can experience intimate love with his or her very best friend.

In the New Testament, Matthew 19: 4-5, Jesus quotes from the Old Testament:

> *He who created them from the beginning made them male and female, and said for this reason a man shall leave his father and mother and cleave to his wife, and the two shall become one flesh.*

The word *cleave* is an interesting Hebrew word that means "absolute unity." Total unity. It is a deeply profound solidarity.

Dr. Tim Keller says that it involves not only a physical union but an emotional union, an economic union and a social union. To cleave to someone is to say, "I completely belong to you. Exclusively! Permanently! Everything I have is yours. I am yours."

This is what marriage is, and this is why God created sex: for cleaving. Sex enables us to truly cleave to another person. God made sex to be able to say to one another, "I belong completely and exclusively and permanently to you. All of me. Everything."

God is completely clear about this—you should never give someone your body if you have not given them your whole self. Otherwise, you are just an object for someone's pleasure. This is why you marry–radically giving yourself, your entire being, unconditionally to someone else. When you follow this prescription, your sex life will soar. When we settle for something less than God's blueprint, sex becomes routine, boring and utterly meaningless.

8.2

How Human Sexuality Impacts a Culture

D R. PETER KREEFT is a brilliant and wise professor who has taught philosophy for more than 48 years, and currently teaches at Boston College.

Approaching the topic of human sexuality, Dr. Kreeft has noted that most people believe there are specific, objective moral laws that we should all follow, but that they are amazingly selective. It always comes down to one area: sex. He believes if Christians would allow the teachings of the Bible on sexuality to be optional, nearly all of the hatred and fear of the church and the Bible would disappear.

Also addressing the subject two years ago, I wrote and published a book on the sexual hookup culture titled, *Sex at First Sight: Understanding the Modern Hookup Culture*. One of the most enlightening truths provided by my research is that when human beings deviate from God's plan for sexuality, it renders a devastating impact on a culture.

Atlanta pastor Andy Stanley points out how most of the major social problems in America are caused by or fueled by the misuse of our sexuality. Take a look at the consequence of teen pregnancy, addiction to pornography, AIDS and other sexually transmitted diseases, abortion, the psychological and physical effects associated with rape, sexual abuse, incest, and all sexual addictions. Perhaps most significant, when you include adultery, which often leads to divorce and the breakup of the family, you can see how out-of-control sex can have far-reaching, damaging consequences to our society.

Stanley makes a great observation. **If we could eliminate all of these sex-related social ills from our society, imagine the resources we would have available to apply to the handful of issues that would remain.**

I also stumbled upon a most curious study from 1934. Prominent scholar J. D. Unwin published a book, *Sex and Culture*. To complete this book, Unwin spent many years closely studying 86 civilizations. His findings startled many people, including Unwin himself, as all 86 demonstrated a direct tie between absolute heterosexual monogamy and the "expansive energy" of civilization. In other words, sexual fidelity was the *single* most important predictor of a society's ascendancy and strength.

Unwin carried no religious convictions and applied no moral judgment.

"I offer no opinion about rightness or wrongness," Unwin said. "In human records, there is no instance of a society retaining its energy after a completely new generation has inherited a tradition which does not insist on pre-nuptial and post-nuptial sexual restraint."

Without a doubt, civilizations flourish when demonstrating premarital sexual restraint, faithfulness and fidelity in marriage. For Roman, Greek, Sumerian, Moorish, Babylonian and Anglo-Saxon civilizations, Unwin studied hundreds of years of history to draw upon, finding no exceptions. These societies flourished culturally and geographically during eras that valued sexual fidelity. Inevitably, sexual standards would loosen, and the societies would subsequently decline, only to rise again when they returned to the more rigid sexual standards.

Unwin seemed at a loss to explain the pattern.

"If you ask me why this is so," Unwin comments, "I reply that I do not know. No scientist does…You can describe the process and observe it, but you cannot explain it."

After reading Unwin's book, Christian author Phillip Yancey offered this:

Unwin preached a message that few people want to hear. Without realizing it, though, Unwin may have subtly edged toward a

Christian view of sexuality from which modern society has badly strayed. For the Christian, sex is not an end in itself, but rather a gift from God. Like such gifts, it must be stewarded according to God's rules, not ours.

Christianity teaches there is a divinely established moral order, and we as human beings just cannot decide for ourselves what is moral. When we choose to defy God's moral order, there is a price we must pay.

If a culture or civilization is no more than a composition of thousands or millions of families, it would stand to reason that each family's teaching and treatment of sex is an important ingredient in not only the family's foundation, but also in the foundation of the larger civilization.

8.3

Sex and the Pursuit of Happiness

OUR VIEWS OF sex and human sexuality have changed dramatically over the last 60 years. If you go back to the 1950s, there was a recognized moral standard when it came to sexual behavior. Sex within marriage was moral and the expected norm. Though people had sex outside of marriage and adultery might have been commonplace, it still was considered to be morally wrong.

That has all changed. Today, for single people, and even for some who are married, sex has gone from being a sacred act between two people in a covenant relationship to nothing more than another form of recreation. It exists for the sole purpose of providing people with pleasure. There is no purpose, meaning or beauty between the two parties involved. Modern people desire to be sexually free, to be liberated to have sex with whomever they please with no strings attached.

Several years ago, Dr. Darrin McMahon, a professor at Florida State University, wrote a landmark book on the history of the pursuit of happiness. In the book, you learn that the more traditional approach to happiness was found by following the path of virtue. Happiness was a by-product of having a strong character.

Dr. McMahon says this is more of an age-old approach, "tying happiness to higher things: to God, virtue, or the right ordering of the soul." Happiness is considered a reward for living well.

Most people know that Thomas Jefferson is the author of the Declaration of Independence. Within the written documents are the famous words that guarantee the rights of all citizens to "Life, Liberty and the pursuit of Happiness."

In reference to the word happiness, Jefferson said, "Happiness is the aim of life, but virtue is the foundation of happiness."

Benjamin Franklin, one of the 56 signers of the Declaration, added, "Virtue and happiness are mother and daughter."

In other words, both men believed you can never find happiness without virtue.

As our country grew, progressed and became more prosperous, a slow transformation took place in our approach to pursuing and finding happiness. Nowadays, much of society believes a life filled with pleasure leads to happiness. Pleasure generally makes us feel good, and good feelings are a major component of living a happy life. For this reason, we equate happiness with pleasure.

It was Sigmund Freud who came along saying that, when you look at people's lives, their only purpose is to be happy and that genital sex is the primary source of all human happiness. Many believe it is Freud's teachings that gave rise to the sexual revolution of the 1960s and have vastly influenced today's view of sex—a culture that believes that sexual pleasure (whether real or imagined in the world of pornography) is essential to our well-being and sense of happiness.

Ironically, what most people do not realize is that Freud's views on sex and sexual boundaries took an apparent shift. He remarked that, when sexual standards disappear, the same thing happens to us that happened "in the decline of ancient civilization, [when] love became worthless and life empty." Surprisingly, Freud actually raised his children with clear-cut sexual boundaries.

Dr. Armand Nicholi, who studied the life of Freud in great detail, says we can only speculate, but Freud resolved in later years that finding happiness in this world requires a great deal of self-restraint.

At this stage in my life, I conclude that pleasure can bring temporary delight into your life, but not lasting happiness. The demand for pleasure is forever at war with reality. It has the potential to enslave you and over time, destroy you.

TO TRULY UNDERSTAND the great transformation that has taken place in our views and beliefs about sexuality, one must go back nearly 2,700 years to a single sentence uttered by the Old Testament prophet Isaiah. His words seem timeless, as if they were written for us today:

> *Woe to those who call evil good, and good, evil; who substitute darkness for light, and light for darkness; who substitute bitter for sweet, and sweet for bitter!" (Isaiah 5:20).*

This is what has happened to us. This is precisely what the media, Hollywood and those who create our entertainment have done. They have taken what God has said is healthy, what is beautiful, and what is good, and they have made it appear to be antiquated, boring and uninteresting. God's laws are in place for a reason, but the secular world minimizes the consequences of sex and overstates its benefits. The secular world has taken what God has said is wrong, evil and unhealthy and has made it appear to be exciting and intriguing.

When was the last time you saw a movie or television program depicting a married couple in a healthy, loving relationship and sex life? Hollywood loves to highlight dysfunctional relationships, infidelity and sex that has no boundaries. People believe this somehow makes for an exciting, magical life.

Another example is how many college students react when they hear the phrase *sexual purity*. Most respond with some wisecrack, particularly if someone suggests the notion. They think the idea is prudish and

✧   ✧   ✧

outdated. But, what the word *purity* means may surprise you.

Christian author Elisabeth Elliott shares a few profound words about purity, particularly in the context of human sexuality:

> *Purity means freedom from contamination, from anything that would spoil the taste or pleasure, reduce the power, or in any way cheapen what the thing was meant to be. It means cleanness; clearness; no additives; nothing artificial; in other words, all natural; in the sense in which the Designer designed it to be.*

In reading this, several words catch my attention—*contamination* and the phrase *reduce the power*. When you think of the future, when you think of your future with your spouse, your soul mate, do you want to risk contaminating and reducing the power of your future sex life? Because this is what is at stake. Reading her message for the first time, I thought, "This is really what I want for my children." Then it struck me.

This is also what I want for my marriage. This is what God offers when we live our lives in harmony with His design.

8.4

The Devastating Consequences of Pornography

THERE IS A WOMAN who shared with me a story of a couple she knew personally. They were newly married, both virgins on their wedding day. Yet, on the first night of their honeymoon, the husband could not perform sexually. He reluctantly confided that he had been hooked on pornography for years. Can you imagine having such an obstacle being thrown into your marriage on your very first day as husband and wife?

In another scenario, we find supermodel Christie Brinkley, considered by many to be one of the most physically attractive women in the world today and featured three times on the cover of *Sports Illustrated Swimsuit Edition*. Brinkley married architect Peter Cook, who was addicted to a $3,000-a-month porn habit, which may or may not have contributed to his affair with a teenager. Cook was married to one of the most beautiful women in the world but still looked to porn to satisfy his sexual desires, destroying his marriage.

An experienced, well-regarded counselor recently told me that pornography is the 500-pound gorilla in the world of addiction. He commented that it is easy to hide from others, is very difficult to overcome, and can have devastating effects on your relationships and your future sex life. Many young men, and even some young women, are graduating from college heavily addicted to pornography. We are only now beginning to understand how pornography influences regular users, particularly those who have viewed it for a number of years.

There are those supporters who argue that pornography has no effect on individuals who consume it, but that's like saying people are not influenced by what they see. The advertising industry will gladly tell you, without question, that what you see enters your mind and heart, impacting who you are and what you do.

Sex therapists and educators Wendy and Larry Maltz authored the well-documented book, The Porn Trap. The writings share how people are shocked when they first hear about the destructive force of pornography. Many consider it to be harmless fun; it's not a drug, alcoholic drink or even an actual sexual experience. So, how can it be so destructive? The Maltzes put it this way:

> *The truth is, using pornography can make you so blind—blind to the power and control it can eventually have over your life.*

Pornography makes a major impact on brain chemistry. It stimulates an area of the brain, known as the "hedonic highway," whereby the chemical dopamine is released when someone is sexually aroused. Pornography causes a huge spike of dopamine production in the brain. Many researchers believe that the dramatic increase in dopamine caused by the viewing of pornography is similar to that of the high someone experiences when using crack cocaine.

The Maltzes further add:

> Porn's power to produce experiences of excitement, relaxation and escape from pain make it highly addictive. Over time you can come to depend on it to feel good and require it so you don't feel bad. Cravings, preoccupations and out-of-control behavior with using it can become commonplace. Porn sex can become your greatest need. If you have been using porn regularly to "get high," withdrawal from porn can be as filled with agitation, depression and sleeplessness, as detoxing from alcohol, cocaine and other hard drugs. In fact, people in porn recovery take an average of 18 months to heal from the damage to their dopamine receptors alone.

Pornography can give an easy escape from real life and all of its pain, but it creates all types of problems, many of which evolve slowly, so you never see them coming until they are serious. The most alarming consequence is that it causes sexual desire and functioning difficulties, and it often shapes one's sexual interests in destructive ways.

Naomi Wolf's *New York* magazine article, "The Porn Myth," posts this:

> You would think porn would make men into raving beasts. On the contrary, the onslaught of porn is responsible for deadening male libido in relation to real women, and leading men to see fewer and fewer women as porn worthy. Women are not having to fend off porn crazed men, but are having a hard time keeping their attention.

Dr. Ursula Ofman, a Manhattan-based sex therapist, has seen many young men coming in to chat about their porn-related issues.

> It's so accessible, and now, with things like streaming video and webcams, guys are getting sucked into a compulsive behavior. What's most regrettable is that it can really affect relationships with women. I've seen some young men lately who can't get aroused with women, but have no problem interacting with the Internet.

Journalist Pamela Paul, in her well-researched book, *Pornified,* says:

> While some men try to keep pornography and real sex separate in their heads, it's not so easy; pornography seeps in, sometimes in unexpected ways. The incursion can even lead to sexual problems, such as impotence or delayed ejaculation.

Sex therapist and psychologist Aline Zoldbrod is convinced that a vast number of young men are destined to be terrible lovers because of pornography. Too many men assume women will respond to them as the porn stars do in the videos. Zoldbrod says they are in for a rude awakening and will make horrible lovers because they do not know how to relate to a real woman.

In her book *What Are You Waiting For?* Dannah Gresh details a common delusion most young people have about pornography: the belief that their issues and problems with porn will go away when they are married. The young women whose fiancés are hooked on porn certainly hope that is true. Gresh says this is the number one question she gets from young people.

"But, the lure of porn is never quenched by marital sex," Gresh adds, "because porn has almost nothing to do with real love and real sex. It's as counterfeit as a counterfeit can be."

In simple terms, author Nate Larkin imparts that pornography corrodes all relationships between men and women because lust kills love. Here is a telling excerpt from Larkin:

> Love gives; lust takes. Love sees a person; lust sees a body. Love is about you; lust is about me and my own gratification. Love seeks . . . knows . . . respects. Lust couldn't care less.

The bottom line is this: Porn satisfies lust, not love. Lust is about me and my own satisfaction. In the end, porn destroys relationships and love. Its impact can be devastating.

❖❖❖

(If you are a parent with teenagers, I want you to know that they have in all likelihood viewed pornographic videos on their smartphone. I encourage you to be very proactive with your children. I challenge parents to put a healthy fear into the lives of their children by continually sharing with them this kind of teaching.)

9

CARE OF THE SOUL

*If there is a God who brought us into existence,
then the deepest chambers of our souls simply cannot be
filled up by anything less than Him.*
~ Augustine

9.1

Care of the Soul

SEVERAL YEARS AGO there was an interview in *The New York Times* where journalist Pat Healy questioned Don Hewitt, who had just ended his 36-year career as the executive producer of "60 Minutes." Healy describes the time spent with Hewitt:

> Hewitt strode into his office and gestured toward the walls. There hung photographs of presidents, diplomats, foreign leaders and entertainers. There were notes from Presidents Reagan and Eisenhower. A constellation of Emmy awards. Arrays of plaques, posters and medallions.
>
> "I'm not trying to be an egomaniacal maniac, but look," he said. "I don't want to lower the temperature. Where the hell do you go? What do you do that's going to be like this?"

Putting it simply, Hewitt had no clue as to what he was going to do with the rest of his life. He realized this flamboyant, exciting journey that he had experienced never resulted in any lasting satisfaction. He was left feeling lost, bewildered.

As you read between the lines, he was able to see that, over the course of this spectacular career, he had neglected his soul. In the interview he admits, "I need to find ways to feed my soul."

A question we should all ask ourselves is, "What is the state of my soul?"

Prominent philosopher Dallas Willard wrote some interesting ideas on the human soul:

> *What is running your life at any given moment is your soul. Not external circumstances, or your thoughts, or your intentions, or even your feelings, but your soul. The soul is that aspect of your whole being that correlates, integrates and enlivens everything going on in the various dimensions of the self. It is the life-center of the human being. It regulates whatever is occurring in each of those dimensions and how they interact with each other and respond to surrounding events in the overall governance of your life. The soul is "deep" in the sense of being basic or foundational and also in the sense that it lies almost totally beyond conscious awareness.*

I find these last words to be vastly significant, that the soul "lies almost totally beyond conscious awareness." For this reason, I am not sure people truly grasp the importance of caring for and properly nurturing the soul. Nor do I think we often recognize the tremendous responsibility we have to guard our souls. As the Apostle Peter challenges us, we are "to abstain from fleshly lusts which wage war against the soul." (I Peter 2:11)

Author John Ortberg includes a special story in his book, *Soul Keeping,* about the importance of protecting the soul:

> There once was a town high in the Alps that straddled the banks of a beautiful stream. The stream was fed by springs that were as old as the earth and as deep as the sea.
>
> The water was clear, like crystal. Children laughed and played beside it; swans and geese swam on it. You could see the rocks and the sand and the rainbow trout that swarmed at the bottom of the stream.
>
> High in the hills, far beyond anyone's sight, lived an old man who served as the keeper of the Springs. He had been hired so long ago that now no one could remember a time when he wasn't there. He would travel from one spring to another in the hills, removing branches or fallen leaves or debris that might pollute the water. But, his work was unseen.

One year the town council decided that they had better things to do with their money. No one supervised the old man anyway. They had roads to repair and taxes to collect and services to offer, and giving money to an unseen stream cleaner had become a luxury that they could no longer afford.

So, the old man left his post. High in the mountains, the springs went untended; twigs, branches and worse muddied the liquid flow. Mud and silt compacted the creek bed; farm wastes turned parts of the stream into stagnant bogs.

For a time, no one in the village noticed. But, after a while, the water was not the same. It began to look brackish. The swans flew away to live elsewhere. The water no longer had a crisp scent that drew children to play by it. Some people in the town began to grow ill. All noticed the loss of sparkling beauty that fed the town. The life of the village depended on the stream, and the life of the stream depended on the keeper.

The city council reconvened, the money was found, and the old man was rehired. After, yet another time, the springs were cleaned, the stream was pure, children played again on its banks, illness was replaced by good health, the swans came home, and the village came back to life.

The life of the village depended on the health of the stream.

The stream is your soul. And you are the keeper.

Reflecting on this beautiful anecdote, the best thing a person can do for the health of his soul is to stay close to and connected to Christ, the Good Shepherd. For we are told that our great tendency is to go astray from Him, go our own way, and eventually end up in the ditch. For this reason, we are reminded of this:

For you were continually straying like sheep, but now you have returned to the Shepherd and Guardian of your souls." (1 Peter 2:25)

9.2

The Two Worlds We Live In

WE LIVE OUR lives in two separate worlds according to Christian author and pastor Gordon McDonald. There is our outer public world, the part of our lives that everyone sees. It is clearly visible, easily measurable, and the part of your life that lets you know if you are successful. Our public life makes great demands on our time and is always pulling at us.

We also have our inner private world. Jesus refers to it as our *innermost being*. This is where we think and reflect. It is where our ideas are formed and our choices are made. Each person's private world is most significantly impacted by our relationship with God.

McDonald conveys it is easy for us to neglect our private world because it is not as visible and demanding. In fact, each of us can ignore our private world for long periods of time, and it is only after these times of neglect that our lives begin to unravel.

I spend most of my work life teaching and counseling businessmen, and have noticed that men size up other men when they meet for the first time. Without realizing it, they compare their lives with others, following a specific blend of criteria:

How does he look and dress?
Where was he educated?
What does he do for a living?

Does he have an impressive title?
What about his wife?
Where does he live?
What kind of car does he drive?
What about this kids? Are they sufficiently accomplished?

If this is the criteria, how well do you measure up?

The problem with this approach is that it is all about the externals. Our lives continue to be measured by our outer, public world. So, you could have a barn full of money, a boatload of talent and movie-star good looks, yet your private, inner world could be a train wreck.

A good example of how we measure external attributes is with Tiger Woods five years ago. As a wise man told me, "Tiger had everything and he traded it for nothing." He had a hole in his soul that he attempted to fill with unbridled sexual experiences. His fans were baffled by this because all they had ever really seen was his outer public life on the golf course. He consistently appeared to be so together. What we did not realize is that his soul was destitute.

The Apostle Paul used insightful words about our public and private worlds:

Therefore we do not lose heart, though outwardly we are wasting away, yet inwardly we are being renewed day by day. (II Corinthians 4:16)

Paul is telling us that, if we are going to live our lives for the externals, we need to know they are wasting away. You see it in your physical body. You see it in your career. It is all passing away. Paul is also implying that, when we live for the externals, we lose heart as time goes by. We leave the world in great despair, and death is ultimately the great enemy; as it removes all of our externals—the things in which we invested our lives.

Notice what Paul says to the Christians at Corinth: "We do not lose heart." The reason for this is because, even though the externals are passing away, our inner life is being renewed and strengthened every day.

This is why Augustine said the following:

If there is a God who brought us into existence, then the deepest chambers of our souls simply cannot be filled up by anything less than Him.

9.3

Strength in Our Innermost Being

D R. CLAYTON CHRISTENSEN is an accomplished fellow. He was a Rhodes Scholar before earning his MBA from Harvard Business School, where he teaches today. He is also the author of five best-selling books.

Christensen has studied and worked with individuals of outstanding merit, ability and character. He has also learned that success does not always happen for those who seem to have the highest potential, making this raw observation of his talented classmates in school:

> My classmates were not only some of the brightest people I've known, but some of the most decent people, too. At graduation they had plans and visions for what they would accomplish, not just in their careers, but in their personal lives, as well. Yet, something had gone wrong for some of them along the way: their personal relationships had begun to deteriorate, even as their professional prospects blossomed. I sensed that they felt embarrassed to explain to their friends the contrast in the trajectories of their personal and professional lives.
>
> At the time, I assumed it was a blip; a kind of midlife crisis. But at our 25- and 30-year reunions, the problems were worse. One of our classmates, Jeffrey Skilling, had landed in jail for his role in the Enron scandal.

Personal dissatisfaction, family failures, professional struggles, even criminal behavior—these problems weren't limited to my classmates at HBS. I saw the same thing happen to my classmates in the years after we completed our studies as Rhodes Scholars at Oxford University. To be given that opportunity, my classmates had to have demonstrated extraordinary academic excellence; superior performance in extracurricular activities such as sports, politics or writing; and significant contributions to their communities. These were well-rounded, accomplished people who clearly had much to offer the world.

But, as the years went by, some of my 32 Rhodes classmates also experienced similar disappointments. One played a prominent role in a major insider trading scandal, as re-counted in the book, *Den of Thieves.* Another ended up in jail because of a sexual relationship with a teenager who had worked on his political campaign. He was married with three children at the time. One who I thought was destined for greatness in his professional and family spheres has struggled in both—including more than one divorce.

I know for sure that none of these people graduated with a deliberate strategy to get divorced or lose touch with their children—much less to end up in jail. Yet, this is the exact strategy that too many ended up implementing.

As you read Christensen's passage, you may wonder how such accomplished and well-rounded individuals who seemingly had everything going for them ended up with extreme personal problems. Through my work with businessmen, I have learned it is easy to focus on our outer, public world while ignoring our inner life, what the Bible often refers to as our soul. This is where these men failed to succeed, neglecting their inner life, causing havoc in their personal lives as a result.

As mentioned in my previous essay, it is easy to become consumed by our outer, public world—the world that is both visible and measurable to others. It is the one part of our lives that people see. The titles, toys and trappings of life are a scorecard of sorts. Our public world is filled with demands upon our time, our money and our energy, making it nearly impossible to ignore.

Our inner life is often neglected as it can be easily ignored; it is not as demanding as our public life. At least, we think that is true until we experience what Gordon McDonald calls a sinkhole-like cave-in. Often, we don't even see it coming.

In the Sermon on the Mount, Jesus delivers a lesson that is pertinent to the sinkhole experience:

> Therefore, everyone who hears these words of mine and puts them into practice is like a wise man who built his house on the rock. The rain came down, the streams rose, and the winds blew and beat against that house; yet it did not fall, because it had its foundation on the rock.
>
> But, everyone who hears these words of mine and does not put them into practice is like a foolish man who built his house on sand. The rain came down, the streams rose, and the winds blew and beat against that house, and it fell with a great crash. (Matthew 7:24-27)

Jesus is telling us that His words and His teaching must flow into our minds and deep down into our souls. We must put into practice everything He teaches us. By doing so, we build a strong foundation for our lives that keeps us from experiencing this sinkhole-like cave-in.

Nurture your soul and establish the care of your innermost being as the top priority in your life. In return, you will develop a strength and stability that will weather even the strongest storms in life.

9.4

Therapy for the Soul

A MONG THE FIRST pioneers to discover the impact emotions play in a person's health was Austrian-Canadian scientist Dr. Hans Selye (1907–1982). On his quest to better understand stress and human emotion, he wrote a total of 30 books on the topics. Toward the end of his life, Dr. Selye summarized all of his research, declaring that anger, bitterness and revenge are the emotions most harmful to our health and well-being. He also concluded that a heart of gratitude is the single most nourishing response that leads to good health. Gratitude and thanksgiving are like therapy for the soul.

If you look closely, you will notice a historical pattern in Western civilization. God blesses certain people who are hardworking, but who are also humble and thankful and depend on God in their day-to-day living. Over time, they experience a certain degree of abundance and wealth.

After time passes, these individuals slowly begin to take credit for all of their prosperity. Their hearts turn to pride and they forget about God. Finally, they descend the slippery slope into the abyss.

Nobel Prize winner Alexander Solzhenitsyn concluded that this is precisely what happened in Russia, sharing:

> Over a half-century ago, while I was still a child, I recall hearing a number of old people offer the following explanation for the great disasters that had befallen Russia: 'Men have forgotten God; that's why all this has happened.'

Since then I have spent well-nigh 50 years working on the history of our revolution; in the process I have read hundreds of books, collected hundreds of personal testimonies, and have already contributed eight volumes of my own toward the effort of clearing away the rubble left by that upheaval. But, if I were asked today to formulate as concisely as possible the main cause of the ruinous revolution that swallowed up some 60 million of our people, I could not have put it more accurately than to repeat: 'Men have forgotten God; that's why all this has happened.'

One of the primary reasons that gratitude is so important is because it is a compound of humility. Truly humble people are grateful people.

In his book, *The Case for Character,* Drayton Nabers provides remarkable insight into the humble life, saying, ". . . humility is a form of wisdom. It is thinking clearly. It is simply being realistic. It is knowing who really deserves the credit and the glory for what we do."

It is an awareness that every good and perfect gift in our lives comes from the hand of God (James 1:17).

There is a brilliant true story in Steven K. Scott's inspiration, "The Richest Man Who Ever Lived":

My former church pastor, Dr. Jim Borror, while visiting a church in the Northwest, was asked by a woman to meet with her husband, a multimillionaire entrepreneur with thousands of employees. Although this man had tens of millions of dollars and everything money could buy, he was unhappy, bitter and cantankerous. No one liked being around him, and contention and strife followed him wherever he went. He was disliked by his employees and even his children. His wife barely tolerated him.

When he met the man, Dr. Borror listened to him talk about his accomplishments and quickly realized that pride ruled this man's heart and mind. He claimed he had single-handedly built his company from scratch. Even his parents hadn't given him a dime. He had worked his way through college.

Jim said, "So, you did everything by yourself."

"Yep," the man replied.

Jim repeated, "No one ever gave you anything."

"Nothing!"

So, Jim asked, "Who changed your diapers? Who fed you as a baby? Who taught you how to read and write? Who gave you jobs that enabled you to work your way through college? Who gave you your first job after college? Who serves food in your company's cafeteria? Who cleans the toilets in your company's restrooms? The man hung his head in shame. Moments later, with tears in his eyes, he said, "Now that I think about it, I haven't accomplished anything by myself. Without the kindness and efforts of others, I probably wouldn't have anything." Jim nodded and asked, "Don't you think they deserve a little thanks?"

That man's heart was transformed, seemingly overnight. In the months that followed, he wrote thank you letters to everyone he could think of who had made a contribution to his life. He wrote thank you notes to every one of his 3,000 employees. He not only felt a deep sense of gratitude, he began to treat everyone around him with respect and appreciation.

When Dr. Borror visited him a year or two later, he could hardly recognize him. Happiness and peace had replaced the anger and contention in his heart. He looked years younger. His employees loved him for treating them with the honor and respect that true humility engenders.

It should strike us all after reading this that humble people are grateful people. They give thanks to those who really deserve the credit. Thanksgiving in one sense is a way we humble ourselves. It is a way to acknowledge that all we are and all we have is a gift from God.

What I have come to realize is that thanksgiving does not come naturally to human beings. We like to take the credit for everything that comes into our lives.

Therefore, a grateful heart is something that has to be cultivated. One has to be intentional about it. This is why I begin each day giving thanks to God. I thank Him for the gift of life, for my wife, my children, and for the other relationships He has blessed me with. I thank Him for the resources He has entrusted me with and the work He has called me to do. Finally, I thank him for the spiritual blessings of life, particularly for His son, Jesus.

Now, as I go through each day, I find myself continually thanking God. I have come to realize this is not only pleasing to Him, but it impacts me. It has changed me. *It is like therapy for the soul.*

10

WISDOM AND A HEALTHY LIFE

My despair came when I compared what I was,
with what I had hoped to be.
~ Mark Twain

10.1

A Reason for Our Discontent

HAVE YOU ever stopped to compare yourself to someone who seems to have it all together? Recently, I read that one of the reasons modern people are unhappy is because they compare themselves to others. Comparison is one way we measure our lives to see how we are doing. We cannot be happy with our lives; we can only be happy relative to how we see others doing in their lives. Without realizing it, this comparison of lifestyles leads to envy.

In the book of Ecclesiastes, we read:

And I saw that all labor and all achievement spring from man's envy of his neighbors.

He is saying that many of us are driven to perform and achieve out of envy.

"Biography" is a television show with each week's episode focusing on a prominent person sharing his or her life story. The show interviews teachers, childhood friends and people who have known the person on the rise to fame.

One of the people recently profiled was Larry Ellison, founder of the wildly successful technology firm, Oracle. Ellison, according to the Forbes 400 list, is the third wealthiest American with a net worth of $53 billion.

While listening to everyone who has known Ellison over the years, it becomes apparent that he is driven primarily by one thing: to surpass Bill Gates' $90 billion first-place status as the wealthiest man in our country.

Ellison's drive is fueled by nothing but envy, which the Bible contends is one of the great evils of life. In fact, the early church recognized it as one of the seven deadly sins. Unfortunately, it runs amok in our lives unnoticed.

Envy literally means to want someone else's life or to want what someone else has. It means to covet, and coveting is forbidden by the Tenth Commandment. When we envy, we consider the person to have a better life than we do. Instead of being happy for the other person, we resent him or we are bitter toward her.

Dr. Tim Keller says the opposite of envy is praise. We rejoice when other people do well and have good things happen to them. Keller suggests that, if you don't believe you are envious of someone, it works in reverse. When the people whom we envy experience failure or have real problems, we secretly rejoice. It makes us happy. The Germans have a word for this: *schadenfreude*, and it means "happiness at the misfortune of others." And yet when others prosper and do really well, their success makes us disappointed and resentful.

Envy clearly has the potential to stab a hole in our souls and drain all of the joy from our lives. Most significantly it can poison our ability to enjoy our present life that God has given us. In turn, this spoils our ability to be grateful for what we have received.

Do you see how this cascades through our lives? If you think about it, we live in a culture that promotes envy. It makes us long to be like the the wealthy, the beautiful, the athletic and the celebrity. It is quite clear that advertisers use envy to motivate us to desire more; mere satisfaction becomes mediocre and is pushed aside. Marketing strategists understand what a strong force envy can be.

In his book, *Lost in the Cosmos: The Last Self-Help Book*, Walker Percy offers simple answers to life's most difficult questions. At one point in the book, he presents a battery of multiple-choice tests to help us understand what is truly going on in our hearts.

It is early morning and you are standing in front of your home, reading the headlines of the local newspaper. Your neighbor of five years, Charlie, comes out to get his paper. You look at him sympathetically—he doesn't take good care of himself and you know he has been having severe chest pains and is facing coronary bypass surgery. But, he is not acting like a cardiac patient this morning!

Over he jogs in his sweat pants, all smiles. He has triple good news! "My chest pains," he crows "turned out to be nothing more than a hiatal hernia, nothing serious." He has also just gotten word of this great promotion he has received and that he and his family will soon be moving to a new home, which happens to be in a much more exclusive part of town. Then, after a pause, he warbles on, "Now I can afford to buy the lake house we have always dreamed of owning."

Once the news settles in, you respond, "That is great, Charlie. I am happy for you."

Now, please fill in the multiple choice. There is only one correct answer to each question.

Question: Are you truly happy for Charlie?

a. Yes, you are thrilled for Charlie; you could not be any happier for him and his family.
b. If the truth be known, you really don't feel so great about Charlie's news. It's good news for Charlie, certainly, but it's not good news for you.

Percy then gives the following directions:

If your answer to the question above is (b), please specify the nature of your dissatisfaction. Do the following thought experiment, which of the following alternative scenarios about Charlie would make you feel better?

a. You go out to get your paper a few days later and hear from another neighbor that Charlie has undergone a quadruple coronary bypass, and that he might not make it.

b. Charlie does not have heart trouble, but he did not get his promotion.

c. As the two of you are standing in front of your homes, Charlie has a heart attack, and you save his life by giving him mouth-to-mouth resuscitation, turning his triple good news into quadruple good news. How happy would that make you?

d. Charlie is dead.

Percy then asks:

Just how much good news about Charlie can you tolerate?

As I noted earlier, envy is not a 21st century phenomenon, yet technology has increased our ability to see into the lives of many more people. Not surprisingly, envy has been elevated as a root cause of personal discontentment. It contributes to why adults find life to be disappointing.

The things we value most are what lead to our envy. If we greatly value money and wealth, we envy those who are very wealthy. If we value business success, we are envious of those in the workplace who are successful.

The Apostle Paul truly understood this. He had been a very wealthy Pharisee prior to his conversion to Christianity. When he became a Christian, he had to sacrifice all of his wealth and power. And yet, he gladly parted with his worldly trappings, as he had found the most valuable possession in all of life, recognizing its value:

> *I consider everything worthless in comparison to the unsurpassing value of Christ Jesus my Lord for whom I suffered the loss of all things, and consider it rubbish so that I might gain this relationship with Christ (Philippians 3:8).*

Paul said this relationship had changed all his worldly ambitions in life. Christianity is not about following a bunch of rules and religious practices. It is about knowing Christ personally and walking through life with Him. Perhaps most importantly, he saw its relative value to all other things. Buoyantly put, they were *rubbish*.

As I get older, the sad truth I find in many people's lives is that they do not *want* God. They might *believe* in Him, they might *seek His favor* by going to church, they certainly *want to be blessed by Him*, but they do *not* want to **know** Him, be close to Him, or allow Him to guide them through life.

Dr. Peter Moore recognized the great value of knowing Christ personally as he reflected on his silver reunion at college:

Returning to my 25th reunion at Yale, I watched as Mercedes-Benz's disgorged prosperous-looking members of the class of 1958 and their wives at the gates of the Old Campus. The program announced that former classmates were preparing to tell the rest of us about the lessons that they had learned while climbing the ladders to success. Wandering along familiar campus pathways that first evening of the reunion, two questions weighed heavily on my mind: "Had I been a success? . . . What was success?" The occasion, redolent with nostalgia, demanded such questions be asked and answers at least attempted. After all, what had one to show for all that expensive education after a quarter of a century?

I tried to be as honest with myself as I could be. I refused to take refuge in pat answers that, after all, I had started this and done that. While I was thus musing, suddenly I remembered that a friend who was a rector of a nearby church had invited me to join him and a handful of parishioners for their customary 5:00 evening prayer. I hurried across campus to St. John's and took my place as the service opened, still very troubled by the questions that I couldn't shake from my mind.

We came in time to join a familiar part of the service, recorded in Luke 2, where the aged Simeon picks up the Christ child in the Temple and blesses God with the words: 'Lord, now lettest thou thy servant depart in peace, according to thy word; for mine eyes have seen thy salvation.' Listening to these words, I felt a quiet assurance settle in my soul. All the anticipation of wise old Simeon's many years found joyous fulfillment in one moment's realization that there in his arms was the long-awaited Messiah. Such was the sense of completeness that his knowledge gave him; he was now ready to 'depart–or die–in peace.'

In the quiet of that service, I discovered what real success was. It came to me quietly, but very clearly, that the only thing worth calling success was coming to the knowledge of God and being able to behold Him in the face of his Son. It seemed to me a knowledge so profound, and yet so simple, that it made even the smallest achievement of great importance when done in its light.

Once our minds and our hearts recognize the true riches of life, and once we see that everything else in this world that people are chasing is not of great value, the envy in our lives will diminish, and we will begin to experience a real contentment in who we are and what we have.

10.2

Slaves of the Past

ONE OF the most popular plays of all time is Thornton Wilder's Pulitzer Prize-winning "Our Town." In one scene, young mother Emily is given the opportunity after she dies during childbirth to go back and observe a single day in her life. She is advised by the dead to choose an "ordinary" day, for even the least important day will be important enough. True enough, Emily chooses a day and quickly finds herself overwhelmed by it. Her ensuing lines are fascinating.

> *I can't go on. It goes so fast . . . I didn't realize. So, all that was going on and we never noticed. Take me back up the hill to my grave. But first, wait! One more look."*
>
> *"Goodbye, goodbye world . . . Mama and Papa. Goodbye clocks ticking . . . and Mama's sunflowers. And food and coffee. And new-ironed dresses and hot baths . . . and sleeping and waking up. Oh, earth, you're too wonderful for anybody to realize you . . .*

Upon returning to the dead, Emily wonders if anyone ever realizes life while they live it—life as it is, "every, every minute" enjoying the present day. The response she receives is pointed. "No . . . the saints and poets, maybe they do some."

I don't know about you, but for me, this is a powerful image and a picture of the Christian view of life. We are to seize each day as it comes and to live one day at a time to its very fullest, because the present day at hand is profoundly important.

In Psalm 118:24, we are told: "This is the day the Lord has made, let us rejoice and be glad in it." It does not say this about yesterday or tomorrow. God calls us to life in the present, content in the now, happy in the now.

I encounter so many people whose lives are haunted by and weighed down by the past. It causes them to live dysfunctionally in the present. It can be a cause of great misery.

God designed us to live a full and joyful life, each day as it comes, with no impediments from the past. Anger, bitterness, hatred, guilt and shame are all about the past. They can enslave us and ruin our lives in the present.

We start by examining anger, bitterness and hatred. In the next essay, we consider guilt and shame.

As we consider the past, it is important to know we are what we remember. The past and what our mind does not let go of does not necessarily determine who we are, but it clearly shapes our life. Furthermore, if we do not recognize the baggage in our life from the past and deal with it, it can sabotage our life now and in the future—particularly in our relationships. Many individuals I encounter are not even aware of how the past has messed up their lives. Those who are aware of it often refuse to deal with it, as the thought of having to deal with the pain from the past can be so frightening that it becomes paralyzing.

Is there anything in your past that is keeping you from living a full and happy life in the present? What about in the life of your spouse? In my work, I often see that when people enter a marriage, it can trigger memories from the past. This is particularly true for those who have been sexually abused.

Anger, bitterness and hatred are linked together in that they are all about the past, where we may have been wronged, injured, abused, mocked or betrayed. But, if people wrong us in any way, we need to know we are responsible for how we respond. We must be aware that anger and bitterness in our lives does not harm anyone but us. In fact, unresolved anger leaves a dark mark on our souls, silently impacting our ability to enjoy life.

I remember reading about John Fogerty and the old rock band

Creedence Clearwater Revival when they had a major falling out, breaking up the band. Fogerty was filled with anger and hatred toward his former band members, so much so that he refused to sing any of their former songs. Many years later, Fogerty realized what his own bitterness was doing to him, reflecting, "Bitterness is a poison you drink, hoping it will cause the other person to die."

It is evident that anger, bitterness and hatred can keep us from experiencing real joy in the present. But, what are we to do about it and how should we respond?

Ultimately, God is the only one who can restore us. In Psalm 23:1–3 we are told:

> The Lord is my shepherd; I shall not want. He makes me lie down in green pastures. He leads me beside still waters. He restores my soul. He leads me in paths of righteousness for his name's sake.

We are told throughout the Bible that God is a *restorer of life*. The word *restore* is a significant word. It means to take something broken, beat up and hurt, and repair it—make it new and whole. Webster's dictionary defines *restore* as, "To bring back or put back into a former or original state." When we are restored, it is as if there has never been any damage done to us.

This is what God wants to do with our past if we allow him.

Anger, bitterness and hatred can enslave our soul. There is only one way to be delivered from it, and that is to forgive. However, forgiveness is counterintuitive. To hate is a much more natural response when we are hurt or wronged by someone.

I now realize that if we are not able to forgive, we have a hard time relinquishing our anger and bitterness. Consequently, we allow those who hurt us to ruin and poison our lives. We give them license to steal our joy, and our anger is doing nothing to hurt them.

In Dr. Tim Keller's book, *Reason for God*, he tells the story of a 16-year-old girl he counseled about the anger she felt toward her father:

> We weren't getting anywhere until I said to her, 'Your father has defeated you as long as you hate him. You will stay trapped in your anger unless you forgive him thoroughly from the heart and

begin to love him.' Something thawed in her when she realized that. She went through the suffering of costly forgiveness, which at first always feels far worse than bitterness, into eventual freedom.

Forgiveness sets us free. As novelist William Young says:

Forgiveness is for the forgiver, to release you from something that will eat you alive, that will destroy your joy and your ability to love fully and freely.

Sometimes when anger is so great toward someone, you may believe there is no way to ever forgive the person. This is when you must look to God for the grace and power to forgive. Confess that you do not have the power to let go of your anger and hatred, and you are looking to Him to enable you to do so. If this is the approach you take and consistently pray to God to help you do what you cannot do yourself, He will begin to work in your life.

Many years ago, I spoke with a woman who was betrayed by her husband. She was angry, badly hurt and had filed for divorce. The problem was that she still loved her husband, and he was deeply repentant. I told her to begin to pray and ask God to enable her to let go of her anger and forgive her husband. I do not remember how long it took, but she was eventually able to forgive him. They reconciled and today have a strong, vibrant marriage. There is power in forgiveness.

Probably the most powerful story I have ever read on the power of forgiveness comes from a letter written to Dr. James Dobson from a woman who listened to his radio program.

In 1991, my beautiful 3½-year-old daughter was accidentally shot in the head and killed by the 8-year-old boy next door. Needless to say, my life came to a screeching halt. My daughter lay dead in the front yard, and my 5-year-old son had witnessed the whole thing. My life went from normal and routine and beautiful to a complete mess, filled with psychiatrists for both my son and myself, near divorce over the next couple years due to the stress, and thoughts of suicide for myself–as well as plotting and planning how I would kill not only the little boy who shot my daughter, but the entire family. I felt justified. I felt that I should do it.

Well, it's been almost four years now. I never did harm the family next door, nor did I harm myself. Instead, I got down on my hands and knees after trying to make it on my own and asked Jesus into my heart. I told Him I wasn't the supermom, super wife, superhuman being that I thought I was. I couldn't do it on my own anymore. Once I prayed that prayer, Jesus started to work in my life. He's still there–so powerfully in fact, that I can almost feel his breath sometimes. He's that close to me.

I had had my tubes tied after my daughter's birth in 1987. In 1992, I went into surgery to have my tubes untied. After several procedures that didn't work, I turned to in vitro fertilization. I was 39 years old when they did the embryo transplant (my egg and my husband's sperm) and implanted five eggs. Three of them adhered to my uterine wall. It was confirmed. I was pregnant with triplets. I can't explain to you how overjoyed I was, not to mention my husband, my family and nearly the whole community where we live, as they were all praying for me.

She goes into great detail to explain the complications of her pregnancy, and how she was advised to abort one of the children, which she refused to do.

Well, I spent my 40th birthday and the next three months after that in bed, drinking two gallons of water every day. On June 11, 1994 (which was the anniversary of when we buried my precious daughter and said goodbye to her for the last time), I gave birth to three absolutely beautiful, perfect boys. Their birth weights were an astonishingly 6 lbs. 14 oz., 6 lbs. 6 oz., and 5 lbs. 8 oz. They never required intensive care. They came home with me in two days, and haven't been sick since they were born nine months ago. "Baby A" is our son Sean Michael. He's gorgeous and full of life. Every time I hold him in my arms, I think that he would have been the one who was most easily accessible.

He's the one we would have lost had I not stood firm on my convictions.

Oh yes, one more thing. I mentioned that God is working so powerfully in my life. Let me just end this letter by telling you that the people next door—the parents of the little boy that killed my little girl—are now the godparents of Sean Michael. Tell me God isn't alive and working in my life.

Jesus has the power to eliminate our anger and hatred, regardless of what has been done to us. John Ortberg says there is only one place you can take your grudges, and that is to the foot of the cross. He adds something we should all take to heart:

At the cross, I remember that I, too, stand in need of forgiveness. At the cross, I remember that for me to expect to receive ultimate forgiveness purchased at the ultimate price from heaven, yet withhold it from someone who has hurt me, is the ultimate contradiction.

10.3

Guilt and Shame

Over the years, I have had the opportunity to see the emotions of guilt and shame surface consistently in people's lives. Both are emotions that involve the past and are linked together in their influence.

They arise from a sense of failure. Guilt on the one hand is a result of moral failure. Shame can also be a result of moral failure, but it can also be the consequence of a failure in, let's say, business, athletics or academics.

Take Tiger Woods for example. Though I don't know this to be true, let's assume he felt a deep sense of guilt after his sexual escapades became front page headlines. He knew he had done wrong, for it was not a behavior taught to him by his parents. So, he felt tremendous guilt. On the other hand, I am sure he felt incredible shame and a sense of dishonor. The shame was tied to letting down all the people who looked up to him.

Today, it would appear the guilt and shame from his moral failure in 2009 have faded, though they may continue to haunt him. There is no way to know for sure. Currently, he is experiencing great shame for his athletic failures. The former number one player in the world is having a difficult time making the cut in many tournaments. I have no doubt he is discouraged, but I would also bet he feels tremendous shame.

Guilt is a result of something you have done. Shame is more focused on who you are. It is to experience a sense of dishonor and indignity. Theologian Lewis Smedes says it is to feel unworthy.

In the 15 seasons of the hit television series "ER," there is one scene that uncomfortably stands out among episodes. A former prison doctor named Truman is in the emergency room, ridden with cancer and laden with guilt. Julia, the chaplain, sits beside him, compassionately listening and being slower to give answers that he would like. One of Truman's roles as a prison doctor was to administer lethal injections to those who were sentenced to die. With great torment, he remembers one man in particular who did not die after the injection and needed to be given a second round. Looking back, Truman believes it was a sign from God, a sign he ignored and would never be able to undo; the man he injected was later found to be innocent, framed for the crime for which he was killed.

Now desperate for answers—blunt and solid answers—Truman reels at Julia for the uncertain comforts she attempts to offer.

"I need answers, and all your questions and your uncertainty are only making things worse!" he yells. But, in his last, livid outburst, he is even more honest. "I need someone who will look me in the eye and tell me how to find forgiveness, because I am running out of time. "

Is there any guilt in your life that resulted from something you did in your past? I recall a 70-year-old man who shared with me a moral failure in his 20s that haunted him all his life. He kept it bottled up, never telling anyone, creating a great burden.

Guilt can torment us unless we know how to deal with it and be released from it. It is critical to know guilt is to the soul what physical pain is to the body. It tells you something is not right in your life, therefore serving as a good thing. However, much depends on what we do with our guilt. If certain behavior causes us to feel guilty, it should lead us to change that behavior. Sometimes it may require us to go to someone and ask for their forgiveness. This can be difficult, but quite liberating.

Finally, it is essential that our guilt be taken to God, where we take our moral failures, confess them and seek His forgiveness. He desires to forgive us, seeing us healed and restored.

Before becoming a Christian, the Apostle Paul was a Pharisee known as Saul of Tarsus, revealing a notorious past. He persecuted the early church, giving approval to the execution of many Christian leaders. After miraculously experiencing an encounter with the risen Christ on the road to Damascus, he became a Christian. Think of Paul's past. I am sure in his missionary journeys he encountered churches and families whose members had been slain or imprisoned by his order.

Clearly the Apostle Paul felt some degree of guilt, to have persecuted the church he had now come to dearly love. So, what did he do? We see from his words in the book of Philippians:

Brethren, I do not yet regard myself as having laid hold of it yet; but one thing I do: forgetting what lies behind and reaching forward to what lies ahead, I press on toward the goal for the prize of the upward call of God in Christ Jesus. (Philippians 3:13, 14)

Paul recognized that, to be truly free to effectively complete the work he was called to do, he had to *forget what lies behind*. Paul dealt with the guilt and shame from his past by experiencing God's forgiveness and redemption. He was clearly not the man he had been and was liberated to press on in his mission.

Paul also recognized, from having been an Old Testament scholar, the depths of God's forgiveness. In the book of Jeremiah God says:

" . . . for I will forgive their iniquity, and their sin I will remember no more."

If God remembered it no more, then neither should we. It is buried in the deepest seas.

Is there any guilt from your past you need to deal with? If so, approach God's throne of grace, and seek His forgiveness with a contrite heart, remembering that not only does He forgive, but He also forgets.

10.4

Satisfying the Desire of the Soul

HAVE YOU ever noticed how once you obtain a possession you have desired for a long time, the joy you receive from it begins to diminish the moment ownership begins? This is true of our achievements, as well. There is no lasting satisfaction.

Next, think of an amazing, pleasurable experience. Once it is over, its euphoria fades. Have you ever stopped to wonder, "Why does this happen?"

New England Patriots quarterback Tom Brady was interviewed on CBS's "60 Minutes" after winning his third Super Bowl a few years ago. Along with his football success, he had plenty of other things our world values: fame, money, dates with supermodels—Brady even married one. Yet, his interview revealed that something was missing.

"Why do I have three Super Bowl rings," Brady said, "and still think there is something greater out there for me? I mean, maybe a lot of people would say, 'Hey, man, this is what it is.' I reached my goal, my dream, my life. Me, I think, '***, it's got to be more than this.' I mean, this isn't, this can't be what it's all cracked up to be."

The interviewer asked, "What's the answer?"

"I wish I knew," answered Brady. "I wish I knew."

It is hard to believe there was no sense of deep satisfaction in Brady's life after reaching his lifetime dream. In fact, he seemed surprisingly bewildered over the emptiness he experienced after this grand achievement. He must have been questioning, "If this does not satisfy me, what will?"

In our innermost being, each of us has a deep yearning that seeks to be satisfied. Unfortunately, most of us are clueless as to what satisfies this strong desire. There are countless types of pleasure, possessions and achievements that can provide it. But, those things never keep their promise.

Sigmund Freud recognized this desire within himself. In a paper he published in 1899, he described it as "a longing that haunted me all of my life." He never was able to satisfy it.

A few of the most insightful words I have ever read on the human search for happiness was in the September 7, 2003, edition of *The New York Times* magazine. A fascinating article, "The Futile Pursuit of Happiness," addressed our mistaken belief of what produces happiness. The article is based on research by Harvard psychology professor Daniel Gilbert and his fellow researchers: psychologist Tim Wilson of the University of Virginia; economist George Loewenstein of Carnegie Mellon University; and the psychologist and Nobel laureate in economics Daniel Kahneman of Princeton University.

When the group searched for the source that produces happiness, it examined the ways we make decisions that we think lead to genuine happiness. Then it examined how people actually felt once they received or experienced what they wanted. Ultimately, it was trying to learn whether our decisions about life give us the emotional happiness we expect.

In the findings, the group began to wonder if everything we have ever thought about life choices, and about happiness, has been at least somewhat naïve and, at worst, greatly mistaken. In other words, we overestimated the actual intensity and duration of our emotional experiences.

As an example, the group mentioned how we might believe an expensive automobile will make us feel wonderful. However, the research shows that such a purchase always turns out to be less exciting than anticipated, lasting for a much shorter period than imagined. Gilbert says it is not that you cannot get the things that make you happy, it just does not give you the thrill you anticipate. Furthermore, the researchers point out that most people do not know what will lead to their ultimate well-being, because our desires bear little relation to the things that truly make us happy.

What I have discovered is that possessions, achievements and pleasurable experiences bring temporary delight into our lives, but not lasting satisfaction. Dr. Tim Keller says, "If you expect this world to give you happiness, you will be utterly disappointed, because you are asking the world to give you something it cannot give."

The reason these words ring true is because this yearning in our innermost being is a spiritual desire of the soul. What we do not seem to realize is that we have a deep thirst in our souls that only God can satisfy.

King David recognized this, which is reflected in his own words from the Psalms:

For He has satisfied the thirsty soul, and the hungry soul He has filled with what is good." (Psalm 107:9)

"As the deer pants for the waterbrook, so my soul thirsts for God." (Psalm 42:1)

Psychiatrist Gerald May observed, "After 20 years of listening to the yearnings of people's hearts, I am convinced that human beings have an inborn desire for God. Whether we are consciously religious or not, this desire is our deepest longing and most precious treasure."

Lawrence Dutton is a member of the classical music ensemble, Emerson String Quartet. He did all the right things for his musical career–started playing early, attended Juilliard and achieved the right accomplishments along the way. One year he and the quartet even won two Grammy awards. It was a remarkable achievement, but Lawrence said that, after the initial euphoria of the awards wore off, he was deeply depressed, as he felt he had done it all. How much higher could he jump?"

Do you see what happened? Dutton was seeking satisfaction in his life through his music, more specifically through musical achievement. It utterly failed him and left him empty and depressed.

Then, something special happened. Dutton became a committed Christian, and everything changed for him. Though he won four more

Grammys, they were inconsequential because he had found and drunk from what the Bible calls "the fountain of living water," experiencing true satisfaction.

It is important to note that Dutton continues to love and play music, and still finds a Grammy award to be a great honor, but he no longer looks for it to satisfy him.

10.5

Moral Confusion

I RECENTLY WATCHED a documentary where a news reporter and a cameraman were conducting man-on-the-street interviews, asking the simple question: *"How do you determine what is right and wrong?"*

Most of the people were dumbfounded by the question and struggled to supply a coherent answer. It struck me as to how modern people are so morally confused.

The reason why is because many individuals believe that moral truth is merely subjective. They think it comes from within the heart, an inner feeling you discover for yourself. "It is my truth. It is true for me, but it might not be true for you."

It is no surprise how this view of morality results in moral confusion. It makes few demands on a person's life. And what should you do when your heart does not speak clearly, and you don't know what to do? How do you get an anchor in your life so you can make wise, moral choices?

For centuries, the Judeo-Christian view of morality was predominant in the western world. This view contends that moral truth is an objective outer reality, revealed by God and, therefore, you submit your life to it. These morals are true for all people, in all places, at all times.

Furthermore, this provides humanity with a moral compass—a moral certainty—so that we have the means to address the confusion we experience all around us. This has been found to be objectively true in the research of a brilliant man, Guenter Lewy.

An author and political scientist, Lewy has been a faculty member at Columbia University, Smith College, and the University of Massachusetts. Back in the early 1990s he set out to write a book on why America does not need religion. He witnessed much of his conservative colleagues taking the position that religion is foundational to morality and social stability. He intended to prove they were wrong, "to make a defense of secular humanism and ethical relativism," he said. In other words, he wanted to prove they were "damned wrong."

After extensive research, the sheer weight of the evidence caused Lewy to change his mind. Instead, with academic integrity, he wrote his book, *Why America Needs Religion,* arguing that religion, particularly Christianity, leads to lower rates of almost every social pathology, including crime, drug abuse, teenage pregnancy and family breakdown. He clearly recognized the positive influence Christianity makes on people's attitudes and intentions. He saw unmistakably how it instills responsibility, moral integrity, compassion and generosity. Lewy concluded:

> *Contrary to the expectation of the Enlightenment, freeing individuals from the shackles of traditional religion does not result in their moral uplift. To the contrary, the evidence now shows clearly that no society has yet been successful in teaching morality without religion.*

Lewy presents a strong argument that biblical morality makes a difference when it is followed out in the real world. The only way to explain the outcome of his research is to recognize that, when people's lives are lined up with the objective structure of God's moral law, they are happier and healthier.

10.6

A Parable

THERE ONCE WAS a prosperous man who set out to build a sailing yacht, intending for it to be the most talked about boat that ever sailed. He spared no expense or effort.

As he created his craft, the man outfitted it with colorful sails, complex rigging and comfortable, plush cabin conveniences. The decks were made from solid teakwood; all the fittings were custom-designed in polished brass. And on the stern, painted in gold letters, readable from a considerable distance, was the name of the boat, *The Persona*.

As he built *The Persona*, the man could not resist fantasizing upon the anticipated admiration and applause from club members at the launching of his new boat. In fact, the more he thought about the praise that was soon to come, the more time and attention he gave to the boat's appearance.

Now—and this seems reasonable—because no one would ever see the underside of *The Persona*, the man saw little need to be concerned about the keel, or, for that matter, anything that had to do with the issues of properly distributed weight and ballast. The boat builder acted with the perceptions of the crowd in his mind–not the seaworthiness of the vessel. Seaworthiness was not a relevant issue while in dry dock.

"Why should I spend money or time on what is out of sight?" he asked himself. "When I listen to the conversations of people at the club, I hear them praise only what they can see. I never recall anyone admiring the underside of a boat. Instead, I sense that my yachting colleagues admire the color and shape of a boat's sails, its brass fittings, its cabin and creature comforts, decks and wood texture, potential speed, and the skill that wins the Sunday afternoon regattas."

And so, driven by such reasoning, the man built his boat. And everything that would be visible to the people soon began to gleam with excellence. But, things that would be invisible when the boat entered the water were generally ignored. People did not take notice of this, or if they did, they made no comment.

The builder's sorting of priorities of resources and time proved to be correct: members of the boat club did indeed understand and appreciate the sails, rigging, decks, brass and staterooms. What they saw, they praised. On occasion, he overheard some remark that his efforts to build the grandest boat in the history of the club would certainly result in his selection as commodore.

When the day came for the maiden voyage, the people of the club joined him dockside. A bottle of champagne was broken over the bow, and the moment came for the man to set sail. As the breeze filled the sails and pushed *The Persona* from the club's harbor, he stood at the helm and heard the admiration he had anticipated for years. The cheers and well-wishes of envious admirers said to one another, "Our club has never seen a grander boat than this. This man will make us the talk of the yachting world."

Soon *The Persona* was merely a blip on the horizon. As it cut through the swells, its builder and owner gripped the rudder with a feeling of fierce pride. What he had accomplished! He was seized with an increasing rush of confidence that everything–the boat, his future as a boat club member (and probably as commodore), and even the ocean–was his to control.

A few miles out to sea, the skies began to unexpectedly darken and a storm arose. It was not a hurricane, but not a squall, either. There were sudden gusts in excess of 40 knots and waves rising above 15 feet. *The Persona* began to shudder, and water swept over the sides. Terrified by the sudden change of the sea, the poise of the captain began to waiver. Perhaps the ocean wasn't his to control after all.

Within minutes *The Persona's* colorful sails were in shreds, the splendid mast was splintered in pieces, and the rigging was unceremoniously draped over the bow. The teakwood decks and the lavishly appointed cabin were awash with water. And before the man could prepare himself, a wave bigger than anything he had ever seen hurled down upon *The Persona*, capsizing the boat.

At this point—and this is important—most boats would have righted themselves after such a battering. *The Persona* did not. Why? Because its builder had ignored the importance of having weight below the waterline. In a moment, when a well-designed keel and adequate ballast might have saved the ship, they were nowhere to be found. The man had concerned himself with the appearance of things and not enough with the needed resilience and stability in the secret, unseen places where storms are withstood.

Furthermore, because the foolish man had such confidence in his sailing abilities, he had never contemplated the possibility of a situation he could not manage. That's why later investigations revealed there were no rescue devices aboard: no rafts, lifejackets or emergency radios. The result of this mixture of poor planning and blind pride was that the foolish man was lost at sea.

Only when the wreckage of *The Persona* was washed ashore did the man's boat-club friends discover his secret.

They proclaimed, "Only a fool would design and build a boat like this, much less sail in it. A man who builds only above the waterline does not realize he has built less than half a boat. Didn't he understand that a boat not built with storms in mind is a floating disaster waiting to happen? How absurd that we should have applauded him so enthusiastically."

The foolish man was never found. Today, when people speak of him—which is rarely—they comment not upon the initial success of the man or the beauty of his boat, but only upon the silliness of setting out on an ocean where storms are sudden and violent. And doing so in a boat not built for anything else but the vanity of its builder and the praise of spectators. It was in such conversations that the owner of *The Persona*, whose name has long been forgotten, became simply known as the foolish man.

As I share this parable with people everywhere, it powerfully speaks into their lives. It is one of the clearest examples of how we can develop such misguided understandings of how to measure our lives. My desire is to challenge everyone to examine how they measure their lives and success; otherwise, we may find ourselves in the same boat as this foolish man.

10.7

The Legacy We Leave Behind

HAVE YOU ever wondered how your life will be remembered once it is over? What will be the legacy you leave behind?

St. Augustine wrote that thinking and reflecting on our legacy is so important, because it helps us think maturely about life, encouraging us to reflect and reconsider who it is we most desire to please.

The issue of legacy can change the course of our lives if we are willing to ask ourselves two related questions: *How do I want to be remembered?* And, *what do I want my life to have been about once it is over?*

Peter Drucker, who is widely considered to be one of the greatest business consultants to ever live, shared that it was thinking about his legacy early in life that shaped him so profoundly as an adult.

> *When I was 13, I had an inspiring teacher of religion, who one day went right through the class of boys asking each one, "What do you want to be remembered for?" None of us, of course, could give an answer. So, he chuckled and said, "I didn't expect you to be able to answer it. But, if you can't answer it by the time you're 50, you will have wasted your life." We eventually had a 16th re-union of that high school class. Most of us were still alive, but we hadn't seen each other since we graduated, and so the talk at first was stilted. Then one of the fellows asked, 'Do you remember Father Pfliegler and that question?' We all did. And each one said it had made all the difference to him, although they didn't really*

understand that until they were in their 40s.

I'm always asking that question: What do you want to be remembered for? It is a question that induces you to renew yourself, because it pushes you to see yourself as a different person–the person you can become.

Drucker says that, once we reflect on how we hope to be remembered, it impacts our entire perspective. As we focus on the type of people we are becoming and how our lives are contributing to the lives of others, it changes the way we measure our lives. Once it finally dawns on us that we will not be remembered for what we have accomplished or what we have achieved or how much money we have made, we acquire the ability to change in a fundamental way.

I think this is what enabled Drucker to turn down Goldman Sachs when he was offered the position to become its chief economist. It was a role that would have paid him a huge salary and thrust him into the international limelight to new heights of fame and glory. But, Drucker had a strong, healthy identity—he knew what he wanted his life to be about, so he turned the offer down.

Recently, I read about Charles Dickens and his famous short novel, *A Christmas Carol.* It was written in 1843, and apparently Dickens was showing us how to live a purposeful life, making a difference in the lives of others.

Ebenezer Scrooge's entire life focused only on money and wealth, caring about them more than anything else in life. In the process, it made him a miserable person, who was viewed with contempt by all who knew him.

However, as the narrative ends, Scrooge's life is transformed as he becomes focused on using his wealth to benefit the lives of others. His life is now full of joyful purpose, and though this is a work of fiction, how do you think Scrooge would be remembered?

We all have a yearning that our earthly lives and endeavors will have some level of permanence that lives on after we are gone. For this to happen, I believe it is imperative to invest in the lives of others. All around us there are those who struggle physically, emotionally and spiritually. Unfortunately, many of us do not want to be troubled by their distresses, as that would personally disturb our lives.

Yet, we must remember that God's priority is people, because people have eternal value. I am reminded of Christian author Max Anders' message:

> *Everything God does is eternally significant. When we are submissive to what He is seeking to accomplish (through us), we find ourselves participating in the eternal.*

This is the key to a lasting legacy and living with a real sense of meaning, knowing that we are participating in the eternal purposes of God.

THE STORMS OF LIFE

The great difficulty spiritually is to concentrate on God, and it is His blessings that make it difficult. Troubles nearly always make us look to God; His blessings are apt to make us look elsewhere.

— Oswald Chambers

Am I Prepared for the Storms of Life?

D R. PAUL BRAND was a world-renowned orthopedic surgeon who wrote about and taught the valuable properties of pain. In his book, *Pain: The Gift Nobody Wants,* he makes this powerful observation:

> My professional life has revolved around the theme of pain, and by living in different cultures, I have observed at close hand diverse attitudes toward it. My life divides roughly into thirds—27 years in India, 25 years in England, and more than 27 years in the United States—and from each society I have learned something new about pain.
>
> I served my medical internship in London during the most harrowing days and nights of the Blitz, when the Luftwaffe was pounding a proud city into rubble. Physical hardship was a constant companion, the focal point of nearly every conversation and front-page headline. Yet, I have never lived among people so buoyant; now I read that 60 percent of Londoners who lived through the Blitz remember it as the happiest period of their lives.
>
> After the war, I moved to India, just as Partition was tearing the nation apart. In that land of poverty and omnipresent suffering, I learned that pain can be borne with dignity and calm acceptance. It was there, too, that I began treating leprosy pa-

tients, social pariahs whose tragedy stems from the absence of physical pain.

Later, in the United States, a nation whose war for independence was fought in part to guarantee a right to the pursuit of happiness, I encountered a society that seeks to avoid pain at all costs. Patients lived at a greater comfort level than any I had previously treated, but they seemed far less equipped to handle suffering and far more traumatized by it. Pain relief in the United States is now a $63 billion-a-year industry, and television commercials proclaim better and faster pain remedies.

Each of these groups—Londoners who suffered gladly for a cause, Indians who expected suffering and learned not to fear it, and Americans who suffered less, but feared it more—helped form my outlook on this mysterious fact of human existence. Most of us will one day face severe pain. I am convinced the attitude we cultivate in advance may well determine how suffering will affect us when it does strike.

In the 1990s, the Public Broadcasting System aired a serious and moving documentary, "Dying," directed and produced by Michael Roemer. In the film, Roemer, who had obtained permission from the patients' families, spent time with several terminally ill cancer victims during their last months of life. The director made this observation after the filming.

"People die in the way they have lived," Roemer said. "Death becomes the expression of everything you are, and you can bring to it only what you have brought to life."

The documentary reveals that those who have prepared for death discover that their final days can be some of life's greatest moments.

This is a question we should all ask. Am I prepared for the storms of life? Am I building a strong supportive life while I am young and healthy? Have I been building a strong foundation as I have been living my life?

In the Sermon on the Mount, Jesus made it clear, warning us in advance that the storms of life are coming. It does not matter who you are. These are His words:

> *"Therefore, everyone who hears these words of Mine and acts on them may be compared to a wise man who built his house on the rock. And the rain fell, and the floods came, and the winds blew and slammed against that house; and yet, it did not fall, for it had been founded on the rock. Everyone who hears these words of Mine and does not act on them, will be like a foolish man who built his house on the sand. The rain fell, and the floods came, and the winds blew and slammed against that house; and it fell— and great was its fall."*

Jesus is instructing us to take God's truth and integrate it into our lives. The central truths of the Bible can serve as a powerful comfort and resource in difficult times. They teach us how to respond to adversity.

In his best-selling book, *Walking with God Through Pain and Suffering,* Dr. Tim Keller offers these insightful words:

> *Once you are in a crisis, there is no time to sit down to give substantive study and attention to parts of the Bible. As a working pastor for nearly four decades, I have often sat beside people who were going through terrible troubles and silently wished they had taken the time to learn more about their faith before the tidal wave of trouble had engulfed them. As we have seen, the main "reasons of the heart" that help us endure suffering are the foundational doctrines of the faith—creation and fall, atonement and resurrection. These are profound and rich truths we need to grasp before we suffer, or we will be unprepared for it. And many of these lessons are very difficult to learn "on the job" when we are in the midst of adversity.*

A great deal of preparation for suffering is simple, but crucial. It entails developing a deep enough knowledge of the Bible and a strong and vital enough prayer life that you will neither be surprised by nor overthrown by affliction.

11.2

Can God Use Pain
to Bless Me?

OVER THE YEARS, I have read a number of C. S. Lewis' insightful books. In the last few years especially, I have read books about his life and the spiritual transformation that took place in the years he was a Christian. Not only was Lewis a brilliant writer, but he was a true man of God.

I recently read a book by Dr. Alister McGrath titled, *If I Had Lunch with C. S. Lewis*. It was an excellent read, exploring a few of Lewis' ideas on some of life's significant issues. I gained new insight on pain and suffering, which he touched upon in his writing.

Most of the atheists in the world today will tell you the number one reason they do not believe in God is because of all the pain and suffering they see around them. How can a loving god allow it? C. S. Lewis was in this camp. If there is no God, the universe is meaningless and, therefore, no explanation for pain and suffering is needed.

But, once Lewis became a Christian, he was forced to think deeply through this issue. One great insight that came to him was the importance of the word "good." What if we confuse the word "goodness" with the word "kindness?" He believed that this confusion is what causes us to approach pain from a false perspective.

Lewis came to believe that we had failed to appreciate what the goodness of God really means. We have developed this idea of a grandfatherly type of figure with a warm, sentimental type of love. We, therefore, have a false, immature view of God.

He says we have to learn to see ourselves as the true objects of God's love. It is a love that comes from an eternal perspective. It is a love that has our best interest at heart, though we cannot often see this or implement it in our own lives.

Suffering generally shows us where we have made poor decisions and choices. It can also point us to the fact that life is transient, and how we desperately need God.

In his book, *The Problem of Pain,* Lewis says, "Pain helps to shatter the illusion that all is well, thus allowing God to plant a flag of truth within the fortress of a rebel soul."

Clearly, as sinful people, our paths need redirecting; there has to be some means for God to accomplish that.

Lewis, in the book, introduces the concept of *the intolerable compliment.* That is, God loves us too much to ignore us. McGrath says, "We would prefer to be left alone, not loved as passionately as this."

Over the years, I have thought a lot about the word "good." What is the ultimate good in life? Most modern people naturally think that it involves prosperity, comfort and having a good time. But, what does God consider to be truly good for our lives?

In Psalm 73:28, we read, "But as for me, the nearness of God is my good." He is telling us that being in close relationship with God is good for his life. The problem is, "All of us, like sheep, have gone astray, each of us has turned to his own way." God, the good shepherd, desires to draw us back to Himself, and sometimes He uses pain as His most effective means."

Several years ago, I had lunch with a man who had survived cancer. He had been given a 50 percent chance of survival, but he did indeed beat the illness. He told me how his business life before the cancer had flourished and he had truly experienced the American Dream. He had everything he wanted in life. And then the cancer came.

As he looked back at his battle with the disease, he told me, "I have come to understand that suffering is good for us." And then he shared why:

1. Suffering causes our minds to focus on what really matters. We so easily are caught up in the trivial.
2. Suffering has deepened my relationship with my wife. Our mar-

riage is at a place it has never been.

3. Suffering has given me a greater burden for people who are hurting.

4. For the first time, Christ is *real* in my life.

What I essentially heard this man saying is that God had made a major breakthrough in his life, and the suffering from cancer was the essential instrument He used to reach him.

11.3

The Painful Circumstances of Life

THE OTHER DAY I ran into a man whom I had not seen in a long time. He looked good and seemed to have his life in order. The next day he sent me an email, sharing with me how much pain he was experiencing in his life. He stopped by my office a few days later, unveiling the painful circumstances of his life.

It made me wonder how many people walk around with smiling faces while their world is falling apart. You never really know.

In talking with this man, I asked him a question that changed the entire dynamic of our conversation. I asked, "Do you think God desires to use these painful circumstances purposefully in your life?"

I am not sure this idea had crossed his mind. I explained to him that if he saw meaning and purpose in his circumstances, it would transform the pain he was experiencing.

The renowned orthopedic surgeon Dr. Paul Brand shares an extremely stark example of how this works out in life. If a woman in love with her husband spends a romantic evening with him and the night ends in sexual intimacy, we can agree this is good for both the man and the woman. This type of intimacy is a wonderful way for couples to express their mutual love.

Now, if we consider the same woman, yet this time she is forcibly raped by a strange man, we cannot possibly imagine there is no definable difference in the experience of such a horrific act from that of having sex with her husband. Physiologically, she experiences the same act involving the same nerve endings. The former experience, however, is one of beauty. The latter is the worst nightmare a woman could imagine. The meaning behind what you are experiencing is everything.

Dr. Henry K. Beecher of Harvard Medical School made an interesting observation among the 215 wounded men from the Anzio beachhead during World War II:

> Only one in four soldiers with serious injuries (fractures, amputations, penetrated chests or cerebrums) asked for morphine, though it was freely available. They simply did not need help with the pain, and indeed many of them denied feeling pain at all. Beecher, an anesthesiologist, contrasted the soldiers' reactions to what he had seen in private practice where 80 percent of patients recovering from surgical wounds begged for morphine or other narcotics.

Here you have two groups of people suffering from the same exact injuries. The soldiers' responses to pain were impacted by the fact that their injuries carried with them a sense of meaning–a result of being involved in a significant mission for their country. They also had a sense of gratitude that they had survived. Yet, the civilian patients with the same exact wounds saw their injuries as being depressing and calamitous, and thus "they begged for morphine or other narcotics."

Just hours before Jesus was taken into custody, He made this point to His disciples in John 16:21:

> *Whenever a woman is in labor, she has pain because her hour has come; but, when she gives birth to the child, she no longer remembers the anguish because of the joy that a child has been born into the world (author paraphrase).*

A woman's pain produces something with great meaning–she has helped create a new life, and for that reason she can contemplate repeating the experience without fear and worry. The point that I am making is crucial to grasp. It is foundational if you are going to deal effectively with painful circumstances.

In the midst of the storms of life, we either allow what we are experiencing to influence our view of God, or we allow our view of God to influence what we are experiencing.

If we will look at the circumstances through the lens of God's truth, how we understand them will be transformed.

Of course this leads to a most obvious question. What do I need to know about God for me to properly interpret what I am experiencing in the storms of life?

I will pick up with that thought in the next essay.

11.4

The Painful Circumstances of Life, Part 2

IN THE last essay, we considered the pain we experience from the storms of life, ending with this thought:

> *In the midst of the storms of life, we either allow what we are experiencing to interpret our view of God, or we will allow our view of God to influence what we are experiencing.*

This leaves us with the natural question, "What do I need to know about God that will enable me to properly interpret the pain I experience?"

I contend there are four important truths that will transform, if not the storms themselves, but how we weather them. But, we must embrace these truths.

Truth #1

In Matthew 6:25, Jesus tells us not to worry about our lives and circumstances. Then in verse 26, He tells us why.

> "Look at the birds in the air, they do not sow or reap or gather into barns, and yet your heavenly Father feeds them. Are you not worth much more than they?

This verse reveals that we are of such great value to God. In Jeremiah

31:3, He tells us that He loves us with an everlasting love.

Therefore, we first need to know that, in the midst of our pain, He has not abandoned us, and He values us greatly.

Truth #2

Jesus tells us in Matthew 10:29, "Are not two sparrows sold for a cent? Yet, not one of them will fall to the ground without your father's consent and notice."

In other words, God is sovereign over all of life. If there is a storm in your life, He has allowed it to come into your life.

Truth #3

In Jeremiah 32:27, we are told, "Behold, I am the Lord, the God of all flesh, is anything too difficult for me?"

God is capable of removing any storm from our lives whenever He chooses. However, if it remains in your life and continues to be there, it is surely there for a reason. Maybe there is purpose in it.

Truth #4

Lastly, we are told in Romans 8:28, "God is causing all things to work together for good to those who love Him and are called according to His purpose."

When I first read this verse, it offered tremendous encouragement, particularly when I realized life was full of difficulty. The problem for me was how to interpret the meaning of "good."

As I mentioned in a previous essay, I have always been intrigued by the word "good" as it relates to our lives. From God's perspective, what is our ultimate good? If you recall, Psalm 73 reveals that being close to God is very good. The Psalmist says, "the nearness of God is my good." It seems logical that, in going through a storm, it is much easier for us to trust God when we are close to Him.

God uses the storms of life to draw us into a closer relationship with Him, which leads to our well-being.

However, as I was thinking about Romans 8:28 and digging further into the text, I soon realized the significance of the next verse in Romans. What I considered to be the good life was not at all what God had revealed it to be. In Romans 8:29, we learn the ultimate good in life is that we be conformed to the image of His son.

This was the exact moment it finally dawned on me that God's desire for me and for all people is to become more like Jesus–increasingly like Jesus. Up until that time, my entire life had focused on what I was achieving and experiencing. God, on the other hand, was more concerned with the type of man I was becoming.

However, as a man, I realized I live in a culture where men do not believe that "Christlikeness" is manly or masculine. Often, men consider that to be like Christ is to be religious, withdrawing from the world.

As I studied Jesus' life, I realized Jesus was not religious–at least, not the way we typically think of as being religious. He lived in a highly religious culture, one where many of the religious people found Him to be contemptible:

- He did not follow their traditions to the letter of the Law.
- Many of the religious leaders did not like the people He hung out with.
- He spoke harshly to the Pharisees and other men of high status and teaching.
- He made political matters worse, as many of their followers began to follow Him and His teachings.

What I now realize is this: Christlikeness is in no way what I thought it to be. In essence, it is:

- To be transformed in our character
- To grow in wisdom
- To love and have compassion
- To build high-quality relationships

Also, as a man, I understand that character, wisdom and love make up the essence of what it means to be an authentic man.

So, I ask you, what is the great good in your life? If it is comfort, prosperity and pleasure, then the storms of life are nothing more than a calamity, which should be avoided at all costs.

However, if the ultimate good in life is to become like Christ, then you will see that God uses the storms of life to bring that to pass. And, therefore, you will see hardship as a blessing—a gift for my ultimate good.

11.5

The Painful Circumstances of Life, Part 3

W E HAVE discussed how life is full of pain and how God uses these storms of life purposefully. We have considered the characteristics of God and the promises He gives to us. These promises can enable us to experience peace when negative circumstances enter our lives. It is here that I address how we should respond when these storms come into clear view, particularly when they are storms in which we have no control.

Some of life's most sacred truths can only be learned as we walk through our individual storms. We all have them. Yet, we only want relief and comfort in the midst of each storm. We demand instant solutions, and we fail to recognize that, although God can solve our problems, instant solutions are not important to Him. What is important to God is how we respond to our struggles.

Often, people instinctively respond to their negative circumstances not only with fear but also with anger and bitterness. "Why me?" they ask. "This is not fair. I don't deserve this!"

Caught up in the process of cursing the realities of life, we more frequently discover that the pain actually continues to increase.

In Philip Yancey's book, *Where Is God When It Hurts?*, he reveals the insight of the highly influential, 20th century Swiss psychologist Paul Tournier.

"Only rarely are we the masters of events," Tournier says, "but [along with those who help us], we are responsible for our reactions."

In other words, we are accountable for the way we respond to the struggles we encounter. Tournier believed that a positive, active and creative response to one of life's challenges develops us, while a negative, angry one only debilitates us, stunting our growth.

In fact, Tournier believed the right response at the right moment might actually determine the course of a person's entire life. He often saw that humans are presented with rare opportunities to develop and grow only through hardship and trial.

Yancey further adds, "That, in fact, was why he [Tournier] moved away from the traditional pattern of diagnosis and treatment and began to address his patients' emotional and spiritual needs as well."

We must all remember that God does not see life and the events of life the way we see them. As the prophet Isaiah informs us, God's thoughts and ways are so much higher than ours.

As mentioned before, Pulitzer Prize-winning author Alexander Solzhenitsyn spent eight years of his life in prison for making a few disparaging remarks about Joseph Stalin. He went into prison as an atheist, yet emerged as a Christian. After he was released, the first words Solzhenitsyn said were this:

I bless you, prison. I bless you for being in my life. For there, lying on the rotting prison straw, I learned the object of life is not prosperity as I had grown up believing, but the maturing of the soul.

How could anyone consider eight years in prison a blessing? Eight years separated from one's family and friends. Solzhenitsyn realized God had made a spiritual breakthrough in his life through prison. A breakthrough that otherwise might never have happened.

If we can see the storms of life as a gift that God is going to use purposefully in our lives for our ultimate good, we can give Him thanks. This requires a tremendous amount of faith, but God always responds to a bold act of faith.

When we are able to trust God with the painful storms of life and by faith, while still believing He is going to use it for our ultimate good, then we can give thanks. When we can express gratitude to God for pain, this is when He unleashes his grace into our lives, and we experience the peace that Paul describes as "passing all understanding."

Faith begets trust, trust delivers gratitude, gratitude produces grace, and finally, grace yields peace—peace, even during the storms when, seemingly, it is at its most valuable.

12

FACING OUR MORTALITY

No philosophy, which will not make sense
of death, is fit to be a guide for life.
~ *Dag Hammarskjold*

Fugitives
from Reality

D R. PETER KREEFT wrote the noteworthy book, *Christianity for Modern Pagans*, a critique of Blaise Pascal's famous book, *Pensees*.

Pensees is a collection of Pascal's arguments defending the Christian faith. He rests his claim on one simple and undeniable fact; that human beings are unhappy. He saw all humans to be on a desperate search for happiness, but were discovering it to be elusive.

Pascal believed that unhappiness is perhaps the most obvious and pervasive feature of the human experience. However, no one wants to talk about it.

There is a clear reason for our unhappiness. According to Pascal, it is because of our mortal condition. Death is the most obvious fact of life. It slaps us in the face when we realize our own helplessness in overcoming it. Deep down we are haunted by the notion that, when we die, we experience the loss of everything in life.

Pascal shares that this is one of the reasons people love pleasure so much. It keeps them from thinking about their mortal condition and the loss of their very being. He says:

> *The only good thing for men, therefore, is to be diverted from thinking of what they are, either by some occupation which takes their minds off it, or by some novel and agreeable passion that keeps them busy, like gambling, hunting, some absorbing show, in short, by what is called diversion.*

Pascal was clearly fascinated by humanity's ability to so easily dodge the realities of life. He believed we are all "fugitives from reality," and that we must be persuaded to have the courage to face the truth about ourselves, our mortality and all the issues that spring from it.

Dr. Thomas Morris, professor of philosophy at the University of Notre Dame, shares a personal story that highlights our obsessive search for diversions to preoccupy our minds. While finishing his graduate training in philosophy at Yale University, Morris had a conversation about work with a young physician, who was finishing his training in pathology.

Soon to enter the job market, Morris asked the new pathologist what the starting salaries were for those who were entering hospital work. The year was 1980, and the doctor indicated he had received several offers well over $100,000.

Not surprisingly, Morris was then asked by the doctor, "What are the salaries like in the academy?" When Morris responded that as a philosophy professor he could expect to be compensated anywhere from $9,000 to $16,000, his friend was staggered.

Since both of them were graduating from Yale and both had worked extremely hard for their degrees and both knew and respected each other's talents, the medical doctor became outraged, his sense of justice and fairness having been grievously assaulted. He knew this man, he knew his abilities.

This story reveals how our society is willing to pay physicians a great deal of money for keeping death and all the issues raised by it at bay. It is not in the least surprising nor objectionable that we are willing to pay dearly for good health.

However, Dr. Morris, in relating this story, makes an important observation when he asks, "Have you noticed that we pay the best entertainers even more, in fact much more [than the doctors]–the movie and television stars, the sports heroes? Maybe it is because we know deep down that the physician will ultimately fail, and the entertainers keep us from thinking about that. This could also explain why we pay philosophers so little: they make us think about it."

The fear of death, unchecked and mismanaged, leads to denial, and in the process, we unconsciously remove truth from its rightful place in our lives. Without truth in our lives, we are lost without a compass.

Pascal warned, "Between us and heaven and hell there is only this life, the most fragile thing in the world."

The fragility of life should force us to become seekers of truth and not drive us deeper into the busyness and the diversions of life. Nowhere will one find that ignorance is a virtue and, contrary to the old adage, it certainly is not bliss.

12.2

If a Man Dies,
Will He Live Again?

N O MATTER how courageous we appear to be or whether we are people of faith or not, human beings always seem to be drawn to this question:

If a man dies, will he live again?

Shakespeare makes a similar observation in "Hamlet." As the main character of this complex tragedy, Hamlet struggles with whether he should end his life. It is at this point in the play that he utters the line, "To be or not to be, that is the question."

In his soliloquy, Hamlet weighs his options. Is it nobler to stay alive and suffer . . . or to go ahead, die and then sleep?

He reasons that, if he takes his own life, he can sleep and end his heartache, but he speculates what might await him beyond the grave. He fears "the dread of something after death."

Hamlet continues to describe death as "the undiscovered country, from whose bourn no traveler ever returns," and he realizes this is what "puzzles the will." Hamlet reasons that we can choose to stay on in this life instead of flying off to some other realm of existence "that we know not of," concluding that the fear of death and the uncertainty of its aftermath makes cowards of us all.

Shakespeare lived in the 16th century, which was described as the "Age of Discovery." It was a time when ships set out to explore distant lands, many of them never returning.

Now imagine you lived in the late 15th century and you were there watching as Columbus set sail to explore the possible distant lands that lay to the west of Europe. But, let's suppose, hypothetically, that Columbus never returned from his voyage. Furthermore, suppose that all the explorers in the 16th century had never returned. At some point, with no one returning after having set sail into the west, exploration of the sea would be very much like death itself—the dark, great unknown.

Eventually, there would be no belief in a distant land because no one had ever returned to describe it. Long voyages out into the sea would be feared and avoided at all costs. Is this not the view of the religious skeptic? There is no afterlife because no one has ever been able to look over into the other side. There is no scientific proof that God and eternal life exist—for if they did exist, would science not have discovered them by now?

Christianity rejects this view of life, because Jesus Christ died a very public death, and three days later returned to demonstrate not only his power over death, but that it is not to be feared. In fact, the New Testament specifically reveals that one of the reasons Christ came into the world was to deliver humanity "from the fear of death, which we are subject to as slaves all of our lives." (Hebrews 2:15)

Jesus has revealed all that we need to know about death and the afterlife. It is crucial to know that God became a man and, most significantly, suffered a human life and death in its fullness, just as each of us will, and He came back to share with us what to expect and what awaits us.

Who else in world history provides such credentials, and who else purports to validate the legitimacy of an afterlife? Who could better provide guidance, greater comfort and a better understanding of life after death? More significantly, the life and death and resurrection of Jesus not only serve as our spiritual foundation, we learn that when we travel to that distant land, He will be with us.

At one point in His teaching, Jesus makes a truly remarkable and astounding statement about Himself. He says "I am the resurrection and the life, he who believes in Me will live even if he dies, and everyone who lives and believes in Me will never die."

It is evident that Jesus came to liberate us from the fear of death and that, through His resurrection, we can find peace and hope as we face our mortality. Clearly, it is His resurrection that can transform a person's approach to life and death. It has happened to countless lives throughout the centuries.

When we consider, for example, the early life of the Russian novelist Leo Tolstoy, who lived in fear of the prospect of his inevitable death, we find he failed to grasp any hope in religion. For many years of his adult life, he deeply pitied the Christians in his native Russia. How was it, he asked, that these miserable, impoverished peasants confronted death with peace and with dignity, content that their days should end and that they would be with their God? A God who doesn't exist?

After many years in the comfort of his aristocratic surroundings—a world of ideas without purpose and privilege without consequence, insulated from the hardships of poverty, physical stress and psychological trauma—Tolstoy's pampered existence slowly began to unravel and eventually he contemplated ending his life at his own hands.

However, his imagination and creative spirit took a radical turn. His life and perspective on death were completely transformed and, ironically, he began to find encouragement and optimism in the community of old, uneducated Christian peasants in his town. He realized they were wiser and more in touch with the realities of human existence than his educated aristocratic friends.

Tolstoy turned to the New Testament. As he searched for the answer, he read the words of Jesus and each page spoke to him lucidly. Over time, by faith, Tolstoy embraced the love of Christ, and as he did, he tells us that the dark menacing figure of death was transformed into the bright promise of life:

> For 35 years of my life I was, in the proper acceptation of the word, a nihilist—not a revolutionary socialist, but a man who believed in nothing. Five years ago, my faith came to me. I believed in the doctrine of Jesus, and my whole life underwent a sudden transformation. Life and death ceased to be evil; instead of despair, I tasted joy and happiness that death could not take away.

12.3

Our Ultimate Hope

IN MY WORK, I have watched scores of men and women struggle with the issue of fear. Living with fear offers a life of anxiety, trauma and unease. A life of peace can only come from the resolution of these anxieties, the removal or changed understanding of that which creates our fears.

Ultimately, the way to deal with fear and uncertainty is to use hope to address the facts. However, when we see the word "hope," it may not instill in us a great deal of confidence, because "hope," unfortunately, is a greatly misunderstood word.

We are poorly served by the manner in which our modern usage of the word has distorted its original meaning. We now employ the word "hope" primarily as a verb, and it loosely connotes uncertainty and an element of wishful thinking. "I hope it does not rain tomorrow."

However, the connotation of the word "hope" that is referred to throughout the Bible is a noun, and it has the semantic meaning of a life-changing certainty of something that has not yet happened, but that we know one day will occur.

Dr. Tim Keller says that we underestimate the power of hope in our lives and just how much our belief in our future determines how we live today. Human beings are clearly hope-based creatures. We are unavoidably shaped by how we view the future, as it impacts the way we process life in the present—the now.

"What we believe about our future," Dr. Keller comments, "is the main determinant in how we process, how we experience, and how we handle circumstances in the present."

Though we might not realize it, we cannot live without hope. Dr. Keller points to Viktor Frankl's noted book, *Man's Search for Meaning*, as an example. Frankl, a Jewish psychiatrist, was one of those fortunate people to survive the Nazi death camps of World War II. As a trained psychiatrist, he was fascinated by why some of his fellow prisoners wasted away and died, while others remained strong and survived. He concluded that we cannot stay healthy if we do not have hope for the future. Frankl writes:

> Life in a concentration camp exposes your soul's foundation. Only a few of the prisoners were able to keep their inner liberty and inner strength. Life only has meaning in any circumstances if we have a hope that neither suffering, circumstances nor death itself can destroy.

Frankl recognized that our believed-in future impacts our ability to cope with our mortality. If our view of the future is grounded in a solid, ultimate hope, then we will have a solid foundation on which to build our lives. However, if our view of the future is rooted in hopelessness, over time we will live with an overriding sense of fear and despair.

Author Philip Yancey shares the story of Allied soldiers in a German prison camp in World War II. They lived in despair, wondering if they would survive and ever see their families again. However:

> Unbeknownst to the guards, the Americans built a makeshift radio. One day news came that the German high command had surrendered, ending the war—a fact that, because of a communications breakdown, the German squads did not yet know. As word spread, a loud celebration broke out.
>
> For three days, the prisoners were hardly recognizable. They sang, waved at guards, laughed at the German shepherd dogs and shared jokes over meals. On the fourth day, they awoke to

learn that all the Germans had fled, leaving the gates unlocked. The time of waiting had come to an end.

If you think about it, nothing had changed in the prisoners' physical circumstances and living conditions, yet they knew the final outcome of the war, and it changed everything.

This is how God intends for his people to live—with great joy as we anticipate the future. He has told us what the final outcome is and what our ultimate destiny is going to be.

As I mentioned in the last essay, Christ came to set us free from the fear of death, which most people are slaves to all of their lives. He tells us the final outcome, and He validates it by Christ's glorious resurrection. This is our ultimate hope. And scripture tells us "this hope is the anchor of our souls." (Hebrews 6:19)

12.4

What Would It Mean If He Really Did Rise?

BORIS PASTERNAK, Russian author and winner of the Nobel Prize in Literature for his novel, *Dr. Zhivago*, was an outspoken atheist for years. Yet, significantly, there came a time in Pasternak's life when he was compelled to confess a profound spiritual confusion.

"I am an atheist," he admitted, "who has lost his faith."

What I have discovered to be highly common is that many atheists like Pasternak find it difficult to live out their faith over a lifetime. This is especially true when they get to the end of their lives and face death.

Former Archbishop of Canterbury Donald Coggan's book, *The Heart of the Christian Faith*, reveals that he was close friends with British philosopher Bertrand Russell. Coggan tells the story of how Russell, as he lay on his death bed, asked Coggan to pray with him. Of course, Russell had historically been an outspoken skeptic of the Christian faith. He is the same man who was once quoted as saying, "When I die, I rot." Yet, in the end, it appears that he, too, may have lost his faith.

Even the godless tyrant, Joseph Stalin, could not seem to shake the presence of God. *Newsweek* magazine quoted Stalin's daughter, Svetlana:

My father died a difficult and terrible death . . . God grants an easy death only to the just. At what seemed the very last moment, he suddenly opened his eyes and cast a glance over everyone in the room. It was a terrible glance, insane or perhaps angry and full of fear of death ... then he lifted his left hand as though he were pointing to something above and bringing down a curse on us all. The gesture was full of menace ... The next moment ... the spirit wrenched itself free of the flesh.

She later said it was as if he were shaking his fist at God in one final act of defiance.

Dr. Samuel Johnson once said, "Depend on it, sir, when a man knows he is to be hanged, it concentrates his mind wonderfully." This is what you see here—men who knew they were dying, and when forced to look into the abyss, were terrorized by fear. For I am convinced that the one question that everyone is asking is: What is going to happen to me after I die?

Author Paul Zahl said it well when he disclosed, "The essence of a religion is to ask what resource it has or doesn't have for a person at the end of his life."

Rollo May, a well-known and highly-regarded therapist, wrote a book several years ago entitled, *My Quest for Beauty*. Perhaps now largely forgotten, the book described his lifelong search for beauty.

May recounts his visit to Mt. Athos, a peninsula in Greece inhabited only by monks from the Greek Orthodox Church. While recovering from a psychological breakdown, he arrived at Mt. Athos just as the monks were celebrating Easter. He vividly describes the deeply symbolic service with its religious icons and ritual and the aroma of incense filling the air.

During the service the priest gave three intricately decorated Easter eggs to each person present. He then pronounced, "Christ is Risen." Everyone in the service, including May, was instructed to respond, "He is risen indeed."

May was not a Christian. Nevertheless, he relates he was profoundly moved by this experience. Seized by a moment of spiritual inspiration, he posed a significant question, "What would it mean for our world if He had truly risen?"

It is critical to think clearly through this question asked by May. What would it mean to my life if Jesus truly rose from the dead? It would mean quite literally everything. It would mean that Jesus is who

He said He was, and it is the living proof that legitimizes His claims of deity. Furthermore, it would mean that Jesus' words and the example of His life have the authority and power to teach us what is true about death and eternity.

If we sincerely believe that Jesus' life and experience and voice are trustworthy, we should then have every right to expect that, when God's everlasting kingdom becomes accessible to us all, it will indeed be more magnificent than anything we could ever imagine.

Blessed be the God and Father of our Lord Jesus Christ, who according to His great mercy has caused us to be born again to a living hope through the resurrection of Jesus Christ from the dead,

To obtain an inheritance which is imperishable and undefiled and will not fade away, reserved in heaven for you. (1 Peter 1: 3, 4)

12.5

Conquering the Fear
of Death

IN HIS PULITZER Prize-winning book, *The Denial of Death*, Ernest Becker says, "The idea of death, the fear of it haunts the human animal like nothing else in all of life."

At the time he wrote this book, Becker was a religious skeptic (although there are some who say he had a change of mind before his death).

It has caused me to question why the religious skeptic, so certain his worldview is true, would have any fear of death at all. He will simply die, falling into an everlasting sleep. Still, it seems that atheists fear death more than anyone else.

For instance, you would expect the father of psychoanalysis, Sigmund Freud, to have had a solid grip on the nature and causes of human psychological weakness in the face of death. In reality, Freud lived with a dreadful fear of death throughout his life. He complained in a letter he once transcribed, "As for me, I note migraine, nasal secretion and attacks of fear of dying."

Ernest Jones wrote a comprehensive biography of Freud's life, pointing out, "Freud seems to have been prepossessed with thoughts about death, more so than any other great man I can think of. He hated growing old, even as early as in his forties, and as he did so, the thoughts of death became increasingly clamorous. He once said he thought of it every day of his life."

Woody Allen, a contemporary movie maker of urbane comedies,

shared his view of life and death as offering no more than "alienation, loneliness and emptiness verging on madness. The fundamental thing behind all motivation and activity is the constant struggle against annihilation and death. It's absolutely stupefying in its terror, and it renders anyone's accomplishments meaningless."

Nineteenth century physician Dr. David Nelson sat at the bedside of numerous patients as they lay dying and would later write about those experiences.

Dr. Nelson gazed into the faces of the terminally ill and watched many of them die with no religious faith, placing a brave face upon their terror. Nelson said, "I could see the fear in their countenance, and it was quite chilling." He witnessed many of them "die cowardly deaths."

Dr. Nelson, who for many years did not believe in God, witnessed the death of Christians, as well. As he looked into their faces, he noted a sense of tranquility, writing "I beheld more celestial triumph than I had ever witnessed anywhere else. In their voice there was a sweetness, and in their eye was a glory that I never would have believed if I had not been there to see it."

Eventually, Dr. Nelson grew a strong faith in Christ, in part because he saw the reality of Jesus in the lives of those dying Christians.

Author Mark Buchanan shares a powerful story from when he was a pastor. It was a late Saturday evening as he read over his sermon for the next morning. Getting into bed later, the phone rang. It was a nurse from the local hospital, speaking frantically. She did not know Buchanan, but he was the only pastor she had heard of in their town, and she faced unfamiliar territory, needing his help.

There was a man at the hospital who was dying. His health was quickly going downhill, and his final moments overflowed with extreme anguish, howling and writhing. The man's family was terrified as they watched. The young nurse begged Buchanan to come to the hospital as fast as he could.

When the pastor arrived at the patient's bedside, he witnessed something he would never forget. The man was twisting, limbs flying everywhere, thrashing and moaning. But, the worst part was the look of terror on this man's face. He was glimpsing hell.

Buchanan did not know what to do, and so he prayed, "God, please help me." He then put his hands on the man and began to pray "shalom," meaning "peace." The dying man began to settle down, his breathing returned to normal, and his body stopped writhing. The man became lucid, and they began to talk.

The pastor asked the man if he knew Jesus Christ. It turned out that, 25 years ago, the man had a spiritual experience, but had never surrendered himself to Christ. Buchanan proceeded to lead the man and his wife into a relationship with Christ. Suddenly, an incredible feeling of peace encompassed the room. The pastor then told the dying man what to expect in God's kingdom. When he left the hospital to head home, he said there was a tangible light and a spirit of celebration in the room.

The next morning after the church service, he stopped by the hospital to see if the man had made it through the night. Pausing at the nurse's station, he was told the man was still alive.

When Buchanan walked into the hospital room, he did not recognize the man. His life had been so transformed that he radiated joy, strength and vitality.

After that day, the pastor never saw the man again. A year later, at the end of another church service, Buchanan was leaving the building when he noticed a woman lingering at the back of the sanctuary. It was the man's wife from the hospital. Buchanan eagerly asked her about her husband. She told him that he had just died last week, although those last few days on earth were the best days of their entire marriage. "He was filled with such joy and peace," she said.

For the Christian, death is not an end, but a transition. Our earthly journey ends at the celestial city, which is vastly more wonderful than this temporary life full of fear, pain and sorrow.

The Christian believes with great confidence that heaven is nothing more than going home to be with our heavenly father.

THE 5 PRINCIPLES

*The lesson of history is that, to the degree people and
civilizations have operated in harmony with correct principles,
they have prospered.*
-- Stephen Covey

1

Sowing and Reaping

A T 18 YEARS of age, Jane Lucretia D'Esterre was a talented and beautiful young woman, entering the prime of her life. As she stood on the bank of a glistening, dark lake in Scotland, she pondered plunging into the depths, taking her life. She had lost all hope. The year was 1815, and her husband, John, had just been killed in a duel. He left her penniless, alone in a new country with two babies to care for. Her family lived in France, so she was without support of any kind: emotional, spiritual or financial.

As she gazed into the rippling waters of the lake and reflected on the pain and brokenness of her life, she looked up and spotted a young man on the other side of the lake, plowing furrows on the hillside. He was completely focused on his work, not aware of her eyes upon him as he guided the plow behind the horse with a single-minded purpose.

In her moment of despair, she was so impressed with the young plowman's focus and concentration to do his work well that his well-timed example pulled her out of her own nightmare. Suddenly, she was infused with hope, receiving a timely dose of wisdom. She knew what she was supposed to do—move straight ahead as the young plowman, as she, too, had a meaningful task to fulfill. Her children needed her. They had lost one parent already and did not need to experience the agonizing loss of another.

When she processed the young man's focus and commitment, she was given wisdom. Or to put it another way, she was given a wise heart. When her heart became wise, it then became brave to do the right thing, which was also the hardest thing to do.

A few weeks after this experience at the lake, Jane came to faith in Christ. Years later, she married Captain John Grattan Guinness, the youngest son of the famous brewer Arthur Guinness.

The prominent author Os Guinness, great-great-grandson of D'Esterre, made this observation:

> If it had not been for the plowman, the tragedy of the dueling husband would have been followed by the tragedy of the duelist's widow.
>
> My great-great-grandmother was unusual for several reasons including the fact that she conscientiously prayed for her descendants down through a dozen generations. Ours is a heritage of faith, which I, for one, am extremely grateful.

When D'Esterre had been a teenager gazing into the deep, dark abyss of the lake, imagining her death, she could not see five generations ahead or any other descendants. All she could feel was that her life was finished. But, it wasn't finished. By looking at a purposeful young man plowing on a hill, she realized there was hope. She could take the path of the lake or she could take the path of moving ahead, in spite of her mind-numbing, emotional pain.

E'Esterre had no idea what the future held nor could she imagine she would ever have another husband who would deeply love her and her children. All she knew at that moment was that she could choose death or life. She had a choice to make that would impact not only her life, her children's lives, but even the lives of her descendants.

Rarely do we fully realize the significance of the decisions and choices we make. They always bring consequences into our lives. It is your choices and decisions that determine the ultimate outcome of your life.

Several years ago, my wife went through a year-long course taught by a fine, well-respected counselor in our city. The purpose was to equip participants with skills needed to help people find healing from the painful struggles of life. The foundation of her lessons and their understanding of people's problems was built on a principle found in one of the letters of the Apostle Paul. In Galatians 6:7, Paul says:

> "Do not be deceived, God will not be mocked, whatever a man sows, this he shall also reap."

Paul uses an illustration from the physical world of agriculture. There are certain objective principles at work in this model, and you have to adapt to them. For instance, if you plant pumpkin seeds, you get pumpkins. If you plant watermelon seeds, you get watermelons. This is the way agriculture works.

This is also true in the spiritual, moral order. Yet, many are blind to this, believing they can live any way they would like without facing the consequences. You cannot just make up the rules for life on the fly. Eventually, there will be grave consequences, as you are out of touch with reality.

You cannot sow pumpkin seeds and get watermelons. You cannot sow foolishly and expect an exceptional life. God makes it clear: "I will not be mocked!" If you sow pumpkin seeds, you are going to get pumpkins. If you sow nothing, you will get nothing. If you sow foolishly, you will reap a life that is impoverished and mediocre.

Notice that Paul also says, "whatever you sow." It is all inclusive. The law of sowing and reaping is functioning in every area of your life including your finances, morals, relationships, physical health, intellect and spiritual life.

This law is operating in your life regardless of your intentions, regardless of how well you understand it, or regardless of whether or not you believe it is true.

The pain and sorrow we often experience is because we break the fabric of God's design and consequently reap what we sow.

Psychologist Chris Thurman wrote an excellent book, *The Lies People Believe*. In the book, he asks:

> "Have you ever noticed how prominent sport stars', businessmen, politicians', and even ministers' lives implode because of scandal and moral failure? In retrospect, in almost every case, we can clearly see the seeds of their downfall sown along the way."

He says they usually begin with a small, seemingly innocuous action here and a careless behavior there. Thurman continues to say that you see:

"Small seeds of moral carelessness sown along life's path that eventually grow into weeds of destruction."

So, I leave you with two questions.

1. "Is there any area in your life where there is a slow erosion or deterioration that is taking place? Most people do not realize that the corruption of our soul happens slowly and imperceptibly over time."

2. "Unless your life is flourishing in all areas, are you willing to sow in a different direction, knowing that every decision and every choice you make will eventually come back to you?"

God is quite clear on this. He will not be mocked. We will, in fact, reap what we sow.

2

Finding Your Center

THERE IS a powerful principle found in Jim Collins' intuitive book, *Good to Great*. It is called "The Hedgehog Principle."

Are you a hedgehog or a fox?

In his famous essay, "The Hedgehog and the Fox," Isaiah Berlin divided the world into hedgehogs and foxes, based upon this ancient Greek parable:

> "The fox knows many things, but the hedgehog knows one big thing." The fox is a cunning creature, able to devise a myriad of complex strategies for sneak attacks upon the hedgehog. Day in and day out, the fox circles around the hedgehog's den, waiting for the perfect moment to pounce. Fast, sleek, beautiful, fleet of foot, and crafty—the fox looks like the sure winner.
>
> The hedgehog, on the other hand, is a dowdier creature, looking like a genetic mix-up between a porcupine and a small armadillo. He waddles along, going about his simple day, searching for lunch and taking care of his home.
>
> The fox waits in cunning silence at the juncture in the trail. The hedgehog, minding his own business, wanders right into the path of the fox.
>
> "Aha, I've got you now!" thinks the fox. He leaps out, bounding across the ground, lightning fast. The little hedgehog, sensing danger, looks up and thinks, "Here we go again. Will he ever

learn?" Rolling up into a perfect little ball, the hedgehog becomes a sphere of sharp spikes, pointing outward in all directions. The fox, bounding toward his prey, sees the hedgehog's defense and calls off the attack. Retreating back to the forest, the fox begins to calculate a new line of attack. Each day, some version of this battle between the hedgehog and the fox takes place, and despite the greater cunning of the fox, the hedgehog always wins.

From this little parable, Berlin divides people into two basic groups: foxes and hedgehogs. Foxes pursue many ends at the same time, viewing the world in all its complexity. They are "scattered or diffused, moving on many levels," says Berlin, never integrating their thinking into one overall concept or unifying vision.

Hedgehogs, on the other hand, simplify a complex world into a single organizing idea, a basic principle or concept that unifies and guides everything. It does not matter how complex the world, a hedgehog reduces all challenges and dilemmas to simple—indeed almost simplistic—hedgehog ideas. For a hedgehog, anything that does not relate to the hedgehog idea holds no relevance.

Princeton professor Marvin Bressler points out the power of the Hedgehog Principle: "You want to know what separates those who make the biggest impact from all the others who are just as smart? They're hedgehogs."

A great question we all should consider is: "Do we have one thing at our core that unifies and guides everything in our lives? Or, are we scattered and diffused with no unifying vision like the fox?

I find that a majority of modern people do not have a spiritual center in their lives and have no idea what they are living for. Consequently, life becomes complex and confusing, with no real sense of meaning.

As you will recall in an earlier chapter, Stephen Covey, in his bestselling book, *The 7 Habits of Highly Effective People,* says that every one of us has a "personal center." Whatever is at the center of our life will be the source of our security, guidance, wisdom and power.

You can see how easily money can work its way to "the center," because we easily believe it can purchase security, power and our ultimate well-being. Over time, however, we discover how money fails us.

It should cause us to wonder if there is something out there at the heart of life that enables us to make sense of it all.

Is there an ultimate security, a true foundation we can build our lives upon? Something that we can truly rely on?

God tells us that He should be that personal center. He desires for us to walk with Him through life as our guide, as our source of wisdom and as our ultimate security.

One who undeniably grasped this concept was C.S. Lewis. He firmly believed that until you allow Christ to be your "personal center," you will never learn who you really are and life will never be truly coherent.

Lewis, in his search for spiritual truth, moved from atheism, to theism and, finally, to the Christian faith. He said that he thought he was finally coming to a place of truth, only to find that the truth itself was a person. Jesus.

In Jesus, C.S. Lewis found the one, single person who could unify and guide his life. In essence, he had found the very center from which all of life flows.

3

One of Life's Most Important Principles

H ANS SELYE was a scientist from Canada who was a true pioneer in discovering the impact of emotions on a person's health, writing more than 30 books on the subject.

In his landmark publication, *The Stress of Life,* Selye's research uncovered a principle that is crucial for a person to have if they are to be emotionally healthy. Creating a fancy term for it, he named it *altruistic egoism.*

As complex as that may sound, it is nothing more than the Biblical truth–"helping others helps you."

In Luke 6:38, Jesus says, "Give and it will be given unto you." In Proverbs 11:25 we are told: "A generous man will prosper; he who refreshes others will himself be refreshed." In other words, when we enrich someone else's life, we find our own lives enriched. Selye observed this principle at work during years and years of research.

This principle in its simplest form states, "We receive in this life by giving." God designed the human heart to give and we receive great joy in this life when we give.

This may sound self-serving to some, that I should give to others so that I can receive. But in reality, God is telling us this is the way I designed you. This is the way you will function best as a human being.

So, if this is true, then the inverse of this principle is also true, that self-centeredness leads to misery in life.

Several years ago, an interesting book was published, selling thousands of copies. "The Narcissism Epidemic," was written by two American psychologists and focused on the significant shift that has occurred in our culture's psychology; the relentless rise of narcissism.

Narcissism is defined as "an excessive interest in oneself and one's physical appearance." The authors contend that this epidemic of narcissism has resulted in people being more depressed, more discontent and more unhappy than ever before.

When we fail to do what God designed us to do, it is just a matter of time before we malfunction.

The story is told by Dr. M. Scott Peck, the famous psychologist and author, who describes a woman patient who suffered from extreme depression. One day, when she was scheduled for an appointment, she called and told Dr. Peck her car had broken down. He offered to pick her up on his way into work, but explained he had to make a hospital call before he got to the office. If she was willing to wait in the car while he made the call, they could have their appointment. She agreed.

When they got to the hospital, he had another suggestion. He gave her the names of two of his patients who were convalescing there, and told her that each of them would enjoy a visit from her. When they met again an hour and a half later, the woman was on an emotional high. She told Dr. Peck that trying to cheer up the patients had lifted her spirits, causing her to feel incredible.

Dr. Peck responded by saying, "Well, now we know how to get you out of your depression. We know the cure for your problem."

The woman answered, "You don't expect me to do that every day, do you?"

When you enrich someone else's life, you find your own life enriched. However, when one is consumed with themselves, it is just a matter of time before they find themselves depleted and emotionally impoverished.

4

The Daffodil Principle

I AM CONVINCED that an exceptional life is determined by how wisely we invest our time.

"The Best Question Ever," written by pastor Andy Stanley, points out there is a cumulative value to investing small amounts of time in certain activities over a long period of time. I would emphasize the combination of two words: "cumulative value."

Cumulative value has application to every area of a person's life. For example, we know there's clearly a cumulative effect if you exercise 35 to 45 minutes a day, five days a week, over a 40-year period. This consistent, disciplined activity is in stark contrast to a sedentary life over that same period of time.

It's important to note, however, that the value of physical exercise is not found in any one particular day. Exercise has a compounding effect. It's the consistent, incremental investment of time that makes a lasting difference.

This is also true if you are investing in relationships, your spiritual life or in your finances. It was Albert Einstein who said, "Compound interest is the most powerful force in the universe."

In Darren Hardy's book *The Compound Effect,* he shares the illustration of the magic penny.

If you were given the choice of receiving $3 million in cash right now or a single penny that would double in value every day for 31 days, which would you choose? Most people impulsively choose the

$3 million in cash. But, if you chose the penny, on day five you would have 16 cents, and on day ten $5.12. After 20 days, with only 11 left, you would have $5,243. This is when the power of compounding begins its rapid ascent. On day 31, you would have $10,737,418.24.

Pennies seem so insignificant, even when they're doubling in value in the first few days. It is only with the passage of time that a paltry penny becomes a vast amount of money. Hardy says few things are as impressive as the magic of compounding pennies, and what we don't realize is that this same compounding force is equally powerful in every area of our lives.

The cumulative effect of investing small amounts of time in carefully chosen activities over a long period can best be understood in *The Daffodil Principle,* created by Jaroldeen Edwards.

Several times my daughter had telephoned to say, "Mother, you must come see the daffodils before they are over." I wanted to go, but it was a two-hour drive from Laguna to Lake Arrowhead. "I will come next Tuesday," I promised, a little reluctantly, on her third call.

Next Tuesday dawned cold and rainy. Still, I had promised, and so I drove there. When I finally walked into Carolyn's house and hugged and greeted my grandchildren, I said, "Forget the daffodils, Carolyn! The road is invisible in the clouds and fog, and there is nothing in the world except you and these children that I want to see bad enough to drive another inch!" My daughter smiled calmly and said, "We drive in this all the time, Mother."

"Well, you won't get me back on the road until it clears, and then I'm heading home!" I assured her.

"I was hoping you'd take me to the garage to pick up my car."

"How far will we have to drive?"

"Just a few blocks," Carolyn said. "I'll drive. I'm used to this."

After several minutes, I had to ask, "Where are we going? This isn't the way to the garage!"

"We're going to my garage the long way," Carolyn smiled, "by way of the daffodils."

"Carolyn," I said sternly, "please turn around."

"It's all right, Mother, I promise. You will never forgive yourself if you miss this experience."

After about 20 minutes, we turned onto a small gravel road and I saw a small church. On the far side of the church, I saw a hand-lettered sign with an arrow that read, Daffodil Garden. We got out of the car and each took a child's hand, and I followed Carolyn down the path. Then, we turned a corner of the path, and I looked up and gasped. Before me lay the most glorious sight.

It looked as though someone had taken a great vat of gold and poured it over the mountain peak and its surrounding slopes. The flowers were planted in majestic, swirling patterns— great ribbons and swaths of deep orange, white, lemon yellow, salmon pink, saffron and butter yellow. Each different-colored variety was planted as a group so that it swirled and flowed like its own river with its own unique hue.

There were five acres of flowers. "But who has done it?" I asked Carolyn. "It's just one woman," Carolyn answered. "She lives on the property. That's her home." Carolyn pointed to a well-kept A-frame house that looked small and modest in the midst of all that glory. We walked up to the house. On the patio, we saw a poster. "Answers to the Questions I Know You Are Asking," was the headline on the sign.

The first answer was a simple one: 50,000 bulbs, it read. The second answer was "One at a time, by one woman. Two hands, two feet, very little brain." The third answer was "Began in 1958."

There it was, The Daffodil Principle. For me, that moment was a life-changing experience. I thought of this woman whom I had never met, who, more than 40 years before, had begun– one bulb at a time –to bring her vision of beauty and joy to an obscure mountaintop. Still, just planting one bulb at a time, year after year, had changed the world. This unknown woman had forever changed the world in which she lived. She had created something indescribable: magnificence, beauty and inspiration.

The principle her daffodil garden taught is one of the greatest principles of celebration. That is, learning to move toward our goals and desires one step at a time–often just one baby-step at time–and learning to love the doing, learning to use the accumulation of time. When we multiply tiny pieces of time with small increments of daily effort, we, too, will find we can accomplish magnificent things. We can change the world.

"It makes me sad in a way," I admitted to Carolyn. "What might I have accomplished if I had thought of a wonderful goal 35 or 40 years ago and had worked away at it 'one bulb at a time' through all those years? Just think what I might have been able to achieve!"

My daughter summed up the message of the day in her usual direct way. "Start tomorrow," she said.

It's so pointless to think of the lost hours of yesterdays. *The way to make learning a lesson of celebration instead of a cause for regret is to only ask, "How can I put this to use today?"*

How do you change the course of your life? How do you live an exceptional life? Learn to use the accumulation of time. Multiply tiny pieces of time with small increments of daily effort and you can accomplish magnificent things.

But, you must put this to use today.

If we do not seize and take hold of our limited time, then our days will continually be devoured by random, unproductive activities that ultimately add up to a lot of wasted time. Novelist Robert Heinlein said, "In the absence of clearly defined goals, we become strangely loyal to performing daily trivia until we become enslaved by it." Because our time is, in fact, our very life, if we waste our time, we will waste our lives.

Furthermore, it is essential to grasp that, if we do not invest regular amounts of time into the important activities of life, the effects of compounding can work in reverse. Neglect is like an ever-growing snowball that has a cumulative negative effect. It can lead to a vicious downward spiral, bringing tremendous pain and disappointment into our lives.

Finally (and it would be impossible to overstate its importance), in the most important areas of your life, you cannot make up for lost time. Never. I remember back in college, friends would goof off during the semester and at exam time, pull all-nighters and cram, hoping to make up for their neglect. Some were able to pull it off; most were not. This strategy does not work in real life. When it comes to relationships, for instance, you can't cram or pull an all-nighter. I've seen this happen in countless marriages. Over the years, some men become less and less attentive to their wives until one day they are stunned when they are served with divorce papers. It is often only then that they are motivated to change their ways. Yet, it is too late, for their wives have decided to move on.

This is equally true in the world of investing. Financially, you cannot wait until you are 60 to start saving for retirement.

The most important areas of your life require regular deposits of time as the years go by. If you miss these opportunities, they are lost forever.

5

To Find Your Life
You Must Lose It

THROUGH ONE of my counseling opportunities, I met several times with a man whom I would describe as an agnostic. He was a bright, well-educated individual, who clearly was searching for spiritual truth. After about six months, he came by my office and announced he was ready to become a Christian. I was so surprised, I nearly fell to the floor.

One of the primary reasons he had come to this decision was that, in his search, much of what he had read in the Bible was counterintuitive. Scriptural teachings went against the grain of natural human instinct and reason. He had concluded that the Bible, and the wisdom of the Bible, could not have been inspired by mere man.

Many of God's important truths are foreign to the world we live in because they are, in fact, counterintuitive. Up seems to be down; down seems to be up. For this reason, Biblical truth comes off as utter foolishness to some people.

What these people do not recognize is that often the wisdom of God, the truth of God, is paradoxical. Paradox is defined in Webster's as: "a tenet that is contrary to received opinion. A statement or principle that is seemingly contradictory and opposed to common sense, but may in fact be true."

A good example of this is where Jesus says, "deny yourself," "die to self," and "lose your life." This teaching is diametrically opposed to a culture that has been raised on slogans like: "Delight yourself," "Indulge yourself," "Grab all the gusto you can," and "If it feels good, do it."

I think this is why certain people are suspicious of Jesus. They see Him as a thief who wants to steal their lives and their happiness.

This is where the paradox of God's truth comes into play. Think about the issue of commitment. Whenever you truly commit to something or someone, you have to give up something in the process. In one sense, you see it as a sacrifice, where you forfeit something of great value for the sake of something of greater value.

In our culture, the commitment we are most aware of is marriage. When a man proposes to a woman, he does so knowing he is giving up all other relationships with women. He is giving up a great deal of his autonomy, as well as all of his assets. When you listen to the marriage vows, you recognize you are giving all that you are and all that you have to that other person. You are telling the person that you belong to him or her exclusively and permanently.

Is this not what we all yearn for? We do it to experience union and oneness with another person, and in the process experience immense joy.

In marriage, when you give up your life, you gain the ultimate human relationship. Jesus is telling us the same thing, that a new, right relationship with Him is worth everything. However, He makes it clear that we must give ourselves to Him, to surrender to Him. And when we do, we will suddenly find everything we have been searching for.

Author Elisabeth Elliott shares a wonderful illustration to help us understand this paradox:

> The growth of all living green things wonderfully represents the process of receiving and relinquishing, gaining and losing, living and dying. The seed falls into the ground, dies as the new shoot springs up. There must be a splitting and a breaking for the bud to form. The bud "lets go" when the flower forms. The calyx lets go of the flower. The petals must curl up and die for the fruit to form. The fruit falls, splits, relinquishes the seed. The seed falls into the ground.

There is no ongoing spiritual life without this process of letting go. At the precise point where we refuse, growth stops. If we hold tightly to anything given to us, unwilling to let it go when its time comes or are unwilling to allow it to be used as the Giver means for it to be used, we stunt the growth of the soul.

Think of your life as an acorn. It is a marvelous little thing, a perfect shape, uniquely designed for its purpose, flawlessly functional. Think of the grand glory of an oak tree. God's intention when he made the acorn was the oak tree.

When you look at the oak tree, you don't feel that the "loss" of the acorn is a great loss. The more you perceive God's purpose in your life, the less terrible the losses seem.

Afterwords

THROUGHOUT my life, I have observed many greatly discouraged men and women who realize the wisdom train has left the station and they are not on board. Sadly, they have been disparagingly misled in their journey and have lost their way.

As you may recall, I shared Seneca's thoughts on wisdom and our need for someone to guide us on our road to find it.

I also cited Solomon's words in Proverbs, "She[Wisdom] is more precious than jewels and nothing you desire compares with her." (3:15)

In the Old Testament, wisdom is often personified; in the New Testament, it is revealed in the person of Jesus Christ.

Colossians 2:3 states that in Christ "are hidden all the treasures of wisdom and knowledge."

We hear from the book of John, "He is the true light that came into the world to enlighten every man and every woman." (1:9)

And Jesus Himself reveals, "I am the light of the world. Whoever follows Me will never walk in darkness but will have the light of life." (John 8:12)

Consider the power of light. One must have it to see both physically and spiritually. The physical realm is distinct and in order to see, three things are necessary: the ability to see, an object to view, and light itself.

These three things are also necessary in the spiritual realm. One uses the mind to see—to understand and distinguish between what is true and what is false. The object to view is spiritual truth; the laws and principles that govern life. And finally, one must have spiritual light. Light reveals what is real, true and good. We desperately need spiritual light to lead healthy, meaningful lives. Again Jesus reminds us, "I am that light."

Alternatively, darkness distorts what is true, meaningful and good. Spiritual darkness prevents us from understanding how life works. In it, we fall, rarely having any idea what we are stumbling over. (Proverbs 4:19)

C. S. Lewis said it best. "I believe in Christianity as I believe that the sun has risen: not only because I see it, but because by it I can see everything else."

Jesus is the ultimate guide in life. In fact, He does not claim to be just any light, but "The Light of the world." He longs to be in a relationship with us throughout the journey, even promising to walk with us "through the valley of the shadow of death." Ask yourself this question: Do I want to walk with Him or do I want to walk alone in the darkness?

Remember, the ultimate outcome of your life is determined by the choices you make. This decision is paramount; therefore make sure you choose wisely.

Acknowledgments and Sources

I AM FIRST and foremost grateful to all of my family, friends, and colleagues here at The Center for Executive Leadership who have encouraged me along the way as I have worked on this project. Most significantly, I want to thank Kim Knott who has worked tirelessly to see this book become a reality.

I would be remiss if I did not acknowledge several individuals whose work greatly influenced the substance of this book. Primarily Tim Keller and Andy Stanley, whose work has profoundly shaped my thinking and perspective on the issue of "wisdom."

Finally, as with any writing, I acknowledge that I am standing on the shoulders of those who have come before me. I offer my deep appreciation to the many people whose writing has informed this work.

Sources

Anders, Max, general editor; Moore, David George and Akin, Daniel L. authors. *Holman Old Testament Commentary, Ecclesiastes, Song of Songs, Holman Reference*. Nashville, TN: Broad man and Holman Publishers, 2003.

Becker, Ernest. *The Denial of Death*. New York, NY: Free Press Paperbacks, Simon 7 Schuster, 1973.

Brand, Dr. Paul and Phillip Yancey. *Pain: The Gift Nobody Wants*. New York, NY: Harper Collins Publishers, Zondervan, 1993, 68.

Brenneman, Greg. *Right Away and All at Once: Five Steps to Transform Your Business and Enrich Your Life.* New York, NY: Rosetta Books, 2016.

Buford, Bob. *Stuck in Half Time: Reinvesting Your One and Only Life,* Grand Rapids, MI: Zondervan Publishing House, 2001, 132–133; and *Finishing Well: What People Who Really Live Do Differently!* Nashville, TN: Integrity Publishers, 2004, 46.

Buford, Bob. *Finishing Well.* Grand Rapids, MI: Zondervan, 2011.

Campolo, Anthony. *The Seven Deadly Sins.* Wheaton, IL: Victor Books, 1987.

Campolo, Tony. *Let Me Tell You A Story.* United States: Thomas Nelson, 2000.

Christensen, Clayton. *How Will You Measure Your Life?* New York, NY: Harper Collins, 2012. United States: Harper Collins, 1986, 51.

Collins, Jim. *Good to Great: Why Some Companies Make the Leap and Others Don't.* New York, NY: Harper Collins Publishers, Harper Business, 2001, 21, 22, 28, 29.

Covey, Stephen R., Merrill, A. Roger, and Merrill Rebecca R. *First Things First: To Live, to Love, to Learn, to Leave a Legacy.* New York, NY: Simon and Schuster, 1994.

Covey, Stephen R. *The Seven Habits of Highly Effective People: Restoring the Character Ethic.* New York, NY: Simon & Schuster, Inc., A Fireside Book, 1989; and with A. Roger Merrill and Rebecca R. Merrill. *First Things First: To Live, to Learn, to Leave a Legacy.* New York: Simon & Schuster, 1994, 50.

Dominguez, Joe and Robin, Vicki. *Your Money or Your Life.* New York, NY: Penguin Group, Inc., 2008.

Easterbrook, Greg. *The Progress Paradox.* New York, NY: Random House, 2003.

Elliot, Elisabeth. *Passion and Purity.* Old Tappan, NJ: Fleming H. Revell Company, 1984.

Farrar, Steve. *How to Ruin Your Life.* Chicago, IL: Thomas Nelson, Inc., 2012.

Fisher, Bob and Fisher, Judy. *Life Is a Gift: Inspiration From the Soon Departed.* New York, NY: Faith Words, Hatchette Book Group, 2008.

Foster, Richard J. *Celebration of Discipline: The Path to Spiritual Growth,* Revised Edition. New York, NY: Harper Collins Publishers, Harper San Francisco, CA, 1988.

Foster, Jerry. *Life Focus: Achieving a Life of Purpose & Influence.* Grand Rapids, MI: Revell Publishing, 2004

Gertner, Jon. "The Futile Pursuit of Happiness." *New York Times* (New York), September 7, 2003: Print.

Gresh, Dannah. *What Are You Waiting For? The One Thing No One Ever Tells You About Sex.* Colorado Springs, CO: WaterBook Press, 2011.

Guinness, Os. *Long Journey Home: A Guide to Your Search for the Meaning of Life.* Colorado Springs, CO: Water Brook Press/Doubleday, 2001, 41.

Guinness, Os. *A Free People's Suicide: Sustainable Freedom and the American Future.* Downers Grove, IL: InterVarsity Press, 2012.

Hagerty, Barbara Bradley. "Quit Your Job." *The Atlantic* (Washington, D.C.), April 2016: Print.

Hall, Laurie. *An Affair of the Mind*. Carol Stream, IL: Wheaton, IL: Tyndale House Publishers, 1996.

Healy, Pat. *"Tell Me a Story: Fifty Years and 60 Minutes in Television."* PublicAffairs (New York). September 7, 2006. Print.

Jeffress, Robert. *The Solomon Secrets*. Colorado Springs, CO: Water-Brook Press, 2002.

Keller, Timothy. *Walking with God through Pain and Suffering*. New York, NY: Dutton, Penguin Group, Inc., 2013.

Keller, Tim. Selected Sermons: "Man in the Wilderness," 1/8/06; "The Wellspring of Wisdom," 9/14/04; "Work and Rest," 3/23/03; "Sickness Upon Death," 9/14/03; "The Search for Pleasure," 9/20/98; "Series on Proverbs," 9/12/04–6/12/05.

Keller, Timothy. *The Reason for God*. New York, NY: Dutton, Penguin Group, Inc., 2008.

Keller, Timothy. *The Meaning of Marriage*. Grand Rapids, MI: Zondervan, 2015.

Knechtle, Cliffe. *Help Me Believe: Direct Answers to Real Questions*. Downers Grove, IL: IVO Books, InterVarsity Press, 2006.

Kreeft, Peter. *Christianity for Modern Pagans*. United States: Ignatius Press, 1993.

Kullberg, Kelly Monroe. *Finding God Beyond Harvard: The Quest for Veritas*. Downers Grove, IL: IVP Books, InterVarsity Press, 2006.

Kullberg, Kelly. *Finding God Beyond Harvard*. Downers Grove, IL: InterVarsity Press, 2006.

L'Abri Fellowship. *What in the World Is Real?: Challenging the Superficial in Today's World*. Champaign, IL: Communication Institute, 1982.

Lewis, C. S. *Mere Christianity: An Anniversary Edition of the Three Books: The Case for Christianity, Christian Behavior, and Beyond Personality*. New York, NY: Macmillan Publishing Co., Inc., 1981.

Lewis, C. S. "The Inner Ring." An Essay. 1944, Print.

Lewis, C. S. *The Problem of Pain*. New York, NY: Harper Collins, 1996.

Lewis, C. S. *Mere Christianity: An Anniversary Edition of the Three Books:* New York, NY: Macmillan Publishing Co., Inc., 1952, 102.

Lewis, C. S. *The Abolition of Man*. New York, NY: Harper Collins, 1974.

MacDonald, Gordon. *The Life God Blesses: Weathering the Storms of Life That Threaten the Soul*. Nashville, TN: Thomas Nelson Publishers, 1994. xx–xxiii.

MacDonald, Gordon. *Ordering Your Private World*. Nashville, TN: Thomas Nelson Publishers, 1985.

Mahan, Brain. *Forgetting Ourselves On Purpose*. San Francisco, CA: Jossey-Bass, John Wiley and Sons, 2002.

Maltz, Wendy and Larry Maltz. *The Porn Trap: The Essential Guide to Overcoming Problems Caused by Pornography*. New York, NY: Harper, 2008.

Marx, Jeffery. *Season of Life: A Football Star, A Boy, A Journey to Manhood.* New York, NY: Simon and Schuster, 2003, 70–73.

Masaryk, Thomas G. *Suicide and the Meaning of Civilization.* Chicago, IL: The University of Chicago Press, 1970.

Maxwell, John. *The 15 Invaluable Laws of Growth.* New York, NY: Hachette Book Group, Inc., 2012.

Maxwell, John C. *The 15 Invaluable Laws of Growth.* New York, NY: Center Street, Hachette Book Group, 2012.

Maxwell, John C. *Today Matters: 12 Daily Practices To Guarantee Tomorrow's Success.* New York, NY: Warner Faith, Time Warner Book Group, 2004.

McGrath, Alister. *The Journey.* New York, NY: Galilee Doubleday, 1999.

McGrath, Alister. *If I had Lunch with C. S. Lewis.* Colorado Springs, CO: Alive Communications, 2014.

McGrath, Alister. *Glimpsing the Face of God: The Search for Meaning in the Universe.* William B. Eerdmans Publishing Company, 2002, 8,9.

McMahon, Darrin M. *Happiness: A History.* New York, NY: Grove Press, 2006.

Meacham, Jon. "From Jesus to Christ." *Newsweek* (United States), March 27, 2005: Print.

Miller, Donald. *Searching for God Knows What.* Nashville, TN: Thomas Nelson, Inc., 2004.

Moore, Peter C. *Disarming the Secular Gods: How to Talk So Skeptics Will Listen.* Downers Grove, IL: InterVarsity Press, 1989, 187-188.

Morris, Tom. *The Art of Achievement: Mastering the 7 C's of Success in Business and Life.* Kansas City, MO: Andrews McMeel Publishing, 2002.

Morris, Tom, Ph.D. *True Success: A New Philosophy Of Excellence.* New York, NY: Berkley, 1994.

Morris, Thomas V. *Making Sense of It All: Pascal and the Meaning of Life.* Grand Rapids, MI: William B. Eerdmans Publishing Company, 1992, 74.

Muggeridge, Malcolm. *A Third Testament.* United States: Ballantine Books, 1983, 58.

Muggeridge, Malcolm. *A Third Testament.* United States: Ballantine Books, 1976, 59.

Nabers Jr., Drayton. *The Case for Character: Looking at Character from a Biblical Perspective.* Tulsa, OK: Christian Publishing Services, 2006.

Nicholi, Dr. Armand M. Jr. *The Question of God: C. S. Lewis and Sigmund Freud Debate God, Love, Sex, and the Meaning of Life.* New York, NY: Free Press, 2002, 115–116.

O'Neil, John R. *The Paradox of Success: When Winning at Work Means Losing at Life: A Book of Renewal for Leaders.* New York, NY: Penguin Putnam Inc., 1993.

O'Neil, John. *The Paradox of Success.* United States: First Trade Paperback Edition, Penguin Group, Inc., 2004.

Ortberg, John. *Soul Keeping.* Grand Rapids, MI: Zondervan, 2014.

Paul, Pamela. *Pornified: How Pornography Is Damaging Our Lives, Our Relationships, and Our Families.* New York, NY: Holt Paperbacks, Henry Holt and Company, 2005.

Pearcey, Nancy R., *Total Truth,* Crossway Books, 2004, p. 60, 61.

Peck, M. Scott, M.D. *The Road Less Traveled: A New Psychology of Love, Traditional Values and Spiritual Growth.* New York, NY: Simon and Schuster, A Touchstone book, 1978.

Roemer, Michael, as quoted in Yancey, Phillip: *Where Is God When It Hurts? A Comforting, Healing Guide for Coping with Hard Times.* Grand Rapids, MI: Zondervan Publishing House, 1990, 260.

Scelfo, Julie. "Men and Depression: Facing Darkness." *Newsweek* (New York), February 26, 2007, 43.

Scott, Steven. *The Richest Man Who Ever Lived.* United States: Crown Business, 2006.

Schwartz, Tony. "What Gets You Up in the Morning?" *New York Times* (New York), May 24, 2013: Print.

Seligman, Martin. *Florish.* New York, NY: Free Press, A Division of Simon and Schuster, Inc., 2011.

Smith, Malcolm. Lecture Series, "The Search for Self-Worth."

Smith, Emily Esfahan. "Meaning is Healthier than Happiness." *The Atlantic* (Washington D.C.). August 2013. Print.

Solzhenitsyn, Alexander. *Gulag Archipelago II.* New York, NY: Harper and Row, 1974, 613-615.

Stanley, Andy. *The Best Question Ever: A Revolutionary Approach to Decision Making.* Colorado Springs, CO: Multnomah Books, 2004

Stanley, Andy. *The Principle Of The Path.* Nashville, TN: Thomas Nelson, Inc. 2008.

Stanley, Andy. *Love, Sex, and Dating.* Grand Rapids, MI: Zondervan, 2014.

Stanley, Thomas and Danko, William. *The Millionaire Next Door.* Lanham, MD: Taylor Trade Publishing, 2010.

Stalin, Svetlana, as quoted in Newsweek, as cited in Tan, Paul Lee, Th.D., *Encyclopedia of 7,700 Illustrations.* Rockville, Maryland: Assurance Publishers, 1979.

Thomas, Gary. *Sacred Marriage.* Grand Rapids, MI: Zondervan, 2015.

Warren, Rick. *The Purpose Driven Life: What on Earth am I Here For?* Grand Rapids, MI: Zondervan, 2002.

Welch, Bob. *52 Little Lessons from a Christmas Carol.* Nashville, TN: Harper Collins Christian Publishing, Inc., 2015.

Willard, Dallas. *Renovation of the Heart: Putting On the Character of Christ.* Colorado Springs, CO: NavPress, 2002, 199.

Williams, Pat. *Coach Wooden's Greatest Secret.* Grand Rapids, MI: Revell 2014.

Wolf, Naomi. "The Porn Myth." *New York Magazine* (New York), October 20, 2003.

Yancey, Phillip. "Christianity Today." March 2005. P.120. Print.

Yancey, Phillip. *Finding God in Unexpected Places.* New York, NY: Doubleday, Random House, 2005.

Yancey, Phillip. *Where Is God When It Hurts? A Comforting, Healing Guide for Coping with Hard Times.* Grand Rapids, MI, Zondervan Publishing House, 1997, 142.

Yancey, Phillip. *Rumors of Another World: What on Earth Are We Missing?* Grand Rapids: Zondervan, 2003.

Yancey, Phillip *Soul Survivor.* Colorado Springs, CO: Doubleday, Random House, Inc., 2003.

Yancey, Phillip. *What Good Is God? In Search of a Faith That Matters.* New York, NY: Faith Words, 2010.

Young, William. *The Shack.* Newbury Park, CA: Windblown Media, 2007.

Whitmen, Meg. "We Need to Intensify Our Sense of Urgency." *Harvard Business Review* (Boston, MA), May 2016, Print.

Author Contact Information

Richard E. Simmons III welcomes inquiries and is available for speaking opportunities to groups, meetings and conferences

For information on scheduling contact:
Jimbo Head at jimbo@thecenterbham.org

Visit our website at:
www.thecenterbham.org

Also by Richard E. Simmons III

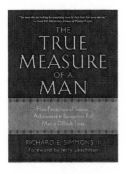

THE TRUE MEASURE OF A MAN
How Perceptions of Success, Achievement & Recognition Fail Men in Difficult Times

In our performance-driven culture this book provides liberating truth on how to be set free from the fear of failure, comparing ourselves to others and the false ideas we have about masculinity.

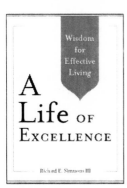

A LIFE OF EXCELLENCE
Wisdom for Effective Living

A Life of Excellence lays out three principles that clearly point to a life of excellence. I am convinced that if one lives in accordance with these principles, their life will flourish and prosper.

– Richard E. Simmons III

SEX AT FIRST SIGHT
Understanding the Modern Hookup Culture

This book explains the hookup culture–how it came about, how it is affecting our younger generation and finally, God's intent for our sexuality.

Also by Richard E. Simmons III

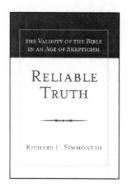

RELIABLE TRUTH

The Validity of the Bible in an Age of Skepticism

Do you believe the Bible is the inspired word of God? Reliable Truth offers powerful and compelling evidence why the Bible is valid and true.

SAFE PASSAGE

Thinking Clearly about Life & Death

Safe Passage examines C. S. Lewis's thoughts and perspective on the issue of human mortality.

REMEMBERING THE FORGOTTEN GOD

The Search for Truth in the Modern World

A fresh, contemporary approach to Christianity, a compassionate yet forceful statement of personal belief.

CPSIA information can be obtained
at www.ICGtesting.com
Printed in the USA
LVOW10*1620010817
543420LV00004B/52/P